the Shot caller

A LATINO GANGBANGER'S MIRACULOUS ESCAPE
FROM A LIFE OF VIOLENCE TO A NEW LIFE IN CHRIST

Casey Diaz

with MIKE YORKEY

EMANATE
BOOKS

Published in Nashville, Tennessee, by Emanate Books, an imprint of Thomas Nelson. Emanate Books and Thomas Nelson are registered trademarks of HarperCollins Christian Publishing, Inc.

Thomas Nelson titles may be purchased in bulk for educational, business, fund-raising, or sales promotional use. For information, please e-mail SpecialMarkets@ThomasNelson.com.

Unless otherwise noted, Scripture quotations are taken from the New King James Version®. © 1982 by Thomas Nelson. Used by permission. All rights reserved.

Scripture quotations marked KJV are from the King James Version. Public domain.

Scripture quotations marked THE MESSAGE are from *The Message*. Copyright © by Eugene H. Peterson 1993, 1994, 1995, 1996, 2000, 2001, 2002. Used by permission of NavPress. All rights reserved. Represented by Tyndale House Publishers, Inc.

Any Internet addresses, phone numbers, or company or product information printed in this book are offered as a resource and are not intended in any way to be or to imply an endorsement by Thomas Nelson, nor does Thomas Nelson vouch for the existence, content, or services of these sites, phone numbers, companies, or products beyond the life of this book.

ISBN 978-0-7852-2452-5 (eBook)
ISBN 978-0-7852-2438-9 (TP)

Library of Congress Control Number: 2018962473

Printed in the United States of America
19 20 21 22 23 LSC 10 9 8 7 6 5 4 3 2 1

To Sana

CONTENTS

FOREWORD

Nicky Cruz

When I read about the life of Casey Diaz, I see so much of my own life.

Growing up as a young boy in Puerto Rico, my family was poor and my parents practiced witchcraft. My father sold out to the devil; my mother sold out to the devil. Me and my brothers and sisters were all subjected to this kind of life. We were cursed.

I became so angry, they sent me to New York City at fifteen to go live with my older brother. I had to fend for myself in a tough, big city.

Casey Diaz was brought to America in a similar way. His parents came from Central America, and he grew up poor on the streets of Los Angeles. He, too, had to quickly learn how to be tough in a big city. Casey had to quickly earn respect in the streets.

Like me, Casey wanted to become the greatest, most violent gang leader he could be. It was a way of gaining a reputation as someone to be feared. He became a leader's leader and he commanded the respect he thought he deserved.

I understand those feelings. When I was in my teens, I was like a wild animal on the streets of New York, so when David Wilkerson came to me in New York and told me about Jesus, me and my friends tried our best to humiliate him and scare him off. But he kept coming. This man had the nerve and the love to penetrate a war zone and tell me about a Jesus I had never heard of.

Even when I threatened to cut him into a thousand pieces, Wilkerson said to me, "Nicky, even if you cut me into a thousand pieces, every one of those pieces will cry out, 'Jesus loves you!'" This man placed himself in the middle of my mess and brought me into the knowledge of Jesus Christ.

I started to wake up and realize Jesus loves Nicky Cruz. Me. I finally surrendered. I fell down crying like a baby, in front of my gang, in front of my friends. I didn't care anymore. I needed to be loved. I was free.

That little boy inside of me—that boy from Puerto Rico who was so hurt—he came alive for the first time. I surrendered all and exchanged my weapons for a Bible. I ate it up. I went to Bible school.

Casey has also experienced the miraculous love of Jesus. What you will read in these pages is a story about a tough young man who lost his way, and the story of a loving God who never forgot Casey, no matter where he was. The Holy Spirit broke through to both of us and gave us new life.

I don't deserve the life I now have. I don't deserve the family and ministry I have been given.

Like the apostle Paul said:

He considered me faithful and trustworthy, putting me into service [for this ministry], even though I was formerly a blasphemer [of our Lord] and a persecutor [of His church] and a shameful and outrageous and violent aggressor [toward believers]. Yet I

was shown mercy because I acted out of ignorance in unbelief.
(1 Timothy 1:12–13 AMP)

God has shown Casey mercy, and it is a beautiful thing. He was ignorant and so was I.

I know you will be inspired by Casey's story. I hope you, too, will surrender to the love of Jesus Christ.

A Note from Casey

What you are about to read is 100 percent true.

Some names have been changed to respect the privacy of individuals mentioned within this book.

Please be aware that I do not seek to glorify or excuse any of the poor choices I made in the past. Instead, my intent is to shine a light on my life as an example of God's redeeming love.

chapter one

IN THE YARD

My cell door swung wide open.

A pot-bellied California correctional officer stood there, jangling a set of keys. "One hour, Diaz," he announced.

Exercise time. For the next sixty minutes, I would be allowed to leave my cell at New Folsom State Prison—where two thousand of California's worst-of-the-worst criminals were locked up—to get some fresh air in the prison yard. I could lift dumbbells, do some chin-ups, or toss a well-worn basketball at the loosest rim west of the Mississippi. Or I could hang out and shoot the breeze with prisoners who were part of my cluster of cells that opened to an indoor communal area inside the prison.

I stood next to my "gate"—that's what we called cell doors in prison—frozen like a statue.

"You coming or going?" the prison guard asked.

On this, my first day with the main prison population, I knew I was supposed to gather the gang leaders together in the exercise yard and share a specific message with them.

"I'm going," I said to the prison guard.

So much had happened in the last twenty-four hours, starting with being transferred from the Security Housing Unit (SHU) inside New Folsom into the general prison population. After three years of solitary confinement—where contact with other humans was severely restricted and generally limited to a mute guard escorting me to the showers or an exercise area—I was now allowed to interact with fellow prisoners in my new surroundings.

This was a big deal since the California prison system knew I was a gang leader from the barrios of downtown LA. The warden was acutely aware that I wasn't someone to trifle with—inside or outside prison walls. I had stabbed people. I had stolen property—from cars to cash to drugs. I had ordered others to take out rival gang members or punks who double-crossed us. I had street cred in spades.

Now I feared the tables had been turned after leaving the solitary confinement found in the SHU, which is pronounced *shoe*. Now that I was part of the general prison population, it was me looking over my shoulder, wary of who was approaching my space.

Dressed in prison-issued blue jeans and a white T-shirt that hung on my five-foot, eight-inch frame that weighed 175 pounds, I fell in with prisoners from our unit of cells as we walked toward the exit leading to an outdoor exercise yard that was as big as a football field. The late-morning sun was comfortable on a spring day in Folsom, approximately twenty miles northeast of Sacramento, the state capital.

I wasn't interested in exercising, because my stomach was tied up in knots. I had a bad feeling about what could happen to me. Yet despite my unsettled equilibrium, I felt an assurance in my heart that I was doing the right thing.

As I was walking out, a half dozen guys materialized out of nowhere and came alongside me. They were Latinos, like me, and definitely in my space. I recognized them as leaders of rival gangs, mostly from Hispanic neighborhoods near downtown Los

Angeles—Pico-Union, Rampart District, MacArthur Park, and South-Central. At one time, we fought bitterly over the same turf, but once we were incarcerated, the distinctions between various Latino gangs vanished. The way things worked in prison, it was the Latinos versus the whites versus the blacks. You stuck with your kind. For protection. To stay alive. And settle scores.

On my way to the yard, they asked how I was doing. From their facial expressions, I could tell they were surprised I had been released from solitary. Prisoners were rarely transferred from the SHU into the main prison population, especially for someone with my status in the gang world.

A tall, skinny dude drew closer. I recognized him from previous prison stints in the LA area. Bullet was his name, and he was clearly the alpha male in the group.

"What's crackin'?" he asked.

"Not much," I replied. "But I have something to tell you and the guys."

I led them to a concrete picnic table, where I sat down on the table-top while the gang leaders gathered around me. They were a bunch of tough-looking dudes. Many sported an array of tattoos declaring their allegiance to MS-13, 18th Street, and Florencia 13.

Bullet looked over his shoulder. Satisfied no guards could over-hear us, he squared his shoulders and faced me.

"So, what is it you want to tell us?" he asked.

Bullet probably expected me to say I wanted to settle a score with another gang member at New Folsom, acquire drugs, or contact someone on the outside. Instead, I gathered myself, knowing what I would say next meant these gang leaders would issue a "green light" on me, meaning I would be killed by another gang member in the very near future.

A murder inside prison walls or outside in the exercise yard was often swift and always brutal. The most popular way of killing someone was jabbing a shank into someone's neck and slicing the jugular vein.

Shanks were crude homemade knives made from scraps of metal, melted plastic, or a piece of wood sharpened like a knife. You could also make a shank from a toothbrush by working the shaft against a piece of metal or a concrete wall until it became a deadly weapon with a sharp point. The bottom of the shank would be tightly wrapped with cloth as a handle, and in the hands of prisoners, they could be used for stabbing another prisoner. They were surprisingly lethal.

The other favored form of killing was strangulation. Prisoners took strands of cloth from boxers, bed sheets, or socks and wove them together until they a became strong, thin rope. While a couple of heavy guys held you down, a third assassin wrapped the handmade cord tightly around your neck and yanked until your oxygen supply was completely cut off. I'd seen such brutal force applied that prisoners were garroted or even beheaded.

Nonetheless, I made eye contact with Bullet and several of the other gang leaders, aware that what I was about to tell them was tantamount to signing my own death warrant.

But I also knew what God wanted me to say.

chapter two

AN IMMIGRANT SON

I can't remember when I came to the United States of America.

That's because I was about two years old when my mom carried me through the border crossing at Calexico, a hardscrabble border town in the middle of California's Sonoran Desert.

The year was 1974. My parents, Rommel Diaz and Rosa Rivas, were not married but were joined together in a common purpose: fleeing their native country of El Salvador for a better life in America, where the streets were paved with gold.

At least, that's the story I heard growing up. For sure, civil war was brewing in El Salvador in the early 1970s, a compact Central America country 140 miles long and 60 miles wide. Since the early 1930s, El Salvador had been ruled by the military with support from the country's landed elite. Known as a coffee republic, 2 percent of the population owned 60 percent of the land. Fourteen families were said to run the country.

When political unrest soared in the early 1970s, secretive death squads comprised of armed paramilitary soldiers—known in Spanish as Escuadrón de la Meurte or "Squadron of Death"—conducted unsanctioned killings or forced disappearances of political opponents, often in the dead of night.

My father had personal experience with the domestic death squads. When he was an eight-year-old boy, in the late 1950s, a band of masked soldiers burst into my grandparents' home one evening with shouts, tipping over furniture and creating a scene. Then they calmly executed my grandfather and my grandmother—who pled for their lives—in front of my father.

That frightening memory always stayed with him. When widespread dissent swelled among the common people in the early 1970s, my parents talked about seeking political asylum in the United States. My mother's sister, Isabelle, wanted to accompany them.

But then my mother became pregnant with me. She felt a prolonged trip via trains and buses would be too difficult. Isabelle still wanted to go, however. After receiving the necessary papers to enter the United States, she made the long trek to Los Angeles, a 2,296-mile journey.

My parents stayed behind in San Salvador, the country's capital, until I was born on November 13, 1972. When their papers to immigrate to the United States finally came through, I was somewhere between eighteen months and two years old. They boarded a train to Mexico City and took a series of bus rides north until we arrived at Mexicali. Their paperwork was in order when they walked across the border and entered the sister city of Calexico. They paid five dollars for their Social Security cards and were told they would eventually receive their green cards.

My parents made their way to Los Angeles and moved to an immigrant neighborhood close to downtown and a pocket of streets known as Koreatown, even though more than 50 percent of the residents were Latino. Our threadbare apartment was located at 9th and Kenmore.

My parents never married, even after they came to Los Angeles. I don't know what their goal was in terms of having a family or building for a future. They lived day to day, part of the mañana philosophy that has seeped into the Latino mind-set: *If something doesn't get done today, there's always tomorrow.*

My mother insisted that I learn English, believing there would be much more opportunity ahead for me if I could speak English fluently. Kids learn quickly on the street, so it wasn't long before I was speaking *Inglés* better than my mother and father. Today, I still speak English much better than Spanish.

My father, hardened by losing his parents in such a brutal manner, was a harsh man. As I grew older and started school, I became aware that he harbored a complete hatred for me. I didn't know what I'd ever done to him, but I distinctly remember sitting at the kitchen table one time when I was six or so. He grabbed me tightly by the shoulders and shook me, saying, "Don't ever call me Papá! I hate you!"

Not only can I recall this incident clearly, but I can still smell the aroma of stale alcohol on his breath. Shaken to my core, I honored his wishes: I never called him Papá—the Spanish equivalent of "Dad"—in my entire life.

When my father wasn't telling me how much he hated me and what a worthless piece of @#$% I was, he would physically assault my mother—sometimes after one of their frequent arguments or sometimes for no reason at all. He'd grab her by the hair and beat the crap out of her. He'd smack her face on furniture or tables and punch her on her back and shoulders. Mom always had a lot of bruises and suffered greatly from the pummelings by my father.

She couldn't fight back. My mother was just a wisp of a woman—five feet, one inch, no more than a hundred pounds. My father was bigger at five feet, seven inches, so while he wasn't physically imposing, he still had a significant height and weight advantage that he viciously used against my mother.

When my father wasn't beating up my mother, they argued about money. My father was a bricklayer but worked only when he felt like showing up at the job. He sold marijuana and other drugs to make a few bucks, but Mom was the main breadwinner—or at least the parent who could be counted on to put food on the table. She toiled as a seamstress at one of LA's notorious downtown sweat shops, sometimes working at two different clothing factories for twelve, fourteen hours a day when money was tight.

Whether my mother worked one or two shifts, I was left alone at home. When my father wasn't working, which was often, he planted himself at a nearby bar, where he drank *cerveza* like spring water. After he got drunk on Coors and Budweiser long-necks—he liked American beer—he'd come home, see me in the living room playing with my toys, and then give me a good whack for no apparent reason.

I tried to exact revenge when I was eight years old. We were in our tiny apartment one night when I found him passed out on the living room floor, lying next to one of those metal, accordion-like heaters hooked up to a gas line. He'd obviously had one too many.

This was my chance to do a number on him. His head was pretty close to the wall heater. I figured that if I opened up the gas valve and let him breathe in the noxious fumes, he'd either get really, really sick or never wake up. Then he wouldn't hit me anytime he felt like it.

First, I had to get his head closer to the gas heater. He was only a few feet away, but if I pushed or dragged his body closer, then he might wake up from his stupor and give me a beating that I'd never forget.

I decided to take that chance. I managed to maneuver my dead-to-the-world father under the gas line. I opened the spigot and let him breathe in the gas while I stepped back and observed what I hoped would be his last breaths. A few minutes passed, but his chest was still rising and lowering.

My mom unexpectedly got home from work. The smell of gas filled the living room, so it took her only two seconds to figure out what was going on.

"What are you doing?" she asked. Her eyes were as big as saucers.

"I don't want him to hurt you anymore. I'll take the blame."

My mother didn't say a thing. She immediately ran to my father's side and shut off the gas valve.

My father never knew how close he came to dying.

I don't know how to really explain this, but I knew at that moment—at eight years old—that I was capable of taking someone's life. Not only was I capable, but it would have been easy for me to do. My father had regularly and ruthlessly beat me up for years, so I had no trouble justifying why he should die. The way I rationalized the situation, life would be better with him out of the picture. The fact that the man lying on the floor was my father didn't even enter into my calculation.

I couldn't understand why my mother didn't take the chance to kill my father. He was the one who made her life so miserable. How many times was she going to allow him to thrash her? Because my father's temper was so volatile, I made sure I spent as much time as I could away from our dingy apartment.

❖ ❖ ❖

Shortly after the gas-line incident, I remember coming home just before dark. We lived on the third floor of our apartment building, which meant there was an elevator, but I preferred to run up the stairs since I was a bundle of energy. We lived in the corner unit at the top of the landing.

At twilight on this particular evening, I reached the top of the stairs and was stunned to see drips of blood leading to our front door. Then I saw a bloody palm print on the front door itself. I knew it was Mom's blood. My father had punched and beaten her again—perhaps within an inch of her life, or worse.

Why hadn't anyone called the police? Mom must have been screaming. She must have been begging my father to stop hitting her. Didn't anyone care?

I carefully opened the front door to our apartment, not knowing what I would find. My heart was beating wildly.

I saw my father first. He was laid out on the dirty carpet, fast sleep. I stepped past him and peeked into the apartment's only bedroom.

"Mom, you there?"

I heard nothing. Then I looked and saw Mom's legs sticking out of the small closet off to the side of the room. I took a few steps for a closer look. She was in a fetal position, holding herself close. Her arms were black and blue, and her hands were bloody. There was crimson blood smeared all over the closet walls.

"Mom, are you okay?"

I didn't receive an answer.

I was so young, I didn't know what to do. I lowered myself and got down next to my mother. I wanted to be close to her. I wanted to protect her, keep her safe in case my father came back to do more damage with his fists of fury. He never returned. When I couldn't keep my eyes open any longer, I fell asleep.

I don't remember what happened in the morning. That memory is blocked from my consciousness. But I do remember thinking, *Man, this is not normal. There's no way this could be normal.*

◆　◆　◆

I had friends at school who laughed and had fun on the schoolyard during recess. I didn't know what joy was. My childhood world was gripped by fear, measured with worry, and surrounded by anxiety. Everywhere I turned, the adults in my life seemed to have it out for me. I remember this one teacher who brought three dozen packages of Thomas English muffins to class one Friday morning and proceeded to hand them out to each student. When she approached my desk, she glanced at me and kept right on walking.

I raised my hand. "Teacher, I didn't get any English muffins," I said. Surely, she had overlooked me.

The teacher, carrying the armload of packages, stopped and met my gaze. "You don't get one," she said coldly. She then continued her delivery round, giving every student a package containing a half dozen Thomas English muffins.

"Wait—what did I do?" I asked as she walked away.

She never looked back.

I was suddenly aware that everyone was looking at me, and I had never felt so alone in my life. I thought I must be a really horrible kid not to get any English muffins like they did.

Another disturbing incident is forever etched in my memory. One evening, while I was sleeping on the living room couch—where I always slept—my father made a huge ruckus as he stormed into our apartment from another night of drinking. The way he was swearing and bumping into stuff told me that he was on another one of his alcohol-fueled binges. He barged into the bedroom, where my mom was sleeping. I listened to cross words and mean things being said. The next thing I heard was *thwack-thwack-thwack* and a body slamming against a wall.

I hopped off the couch, dressed in briefs and a T-shirt. When I stepped into their bedroom, I saw my father standing over my mother with fist raised. Mom was lying on the floor, clearly in pain.

"Run," my mother whispered through cracked lips. "Run. Go get help."

I wanted to alleviate her pain. I wanted her to be safe.

"Okay, Mom. I will."

At eight years old, I didn't really know how to "go get help." But I knew enough to realize that any sort of assistance would have to come from outside the four thin walls of our apartment.

I opened the front door and sprinted down three flights of stairs to 9th Street, still wearing my T-shirt and briefs. I felt the cold of the midwinter evening and wondered if I had done the right thing by leaving a relatively warm apartment. I sat down on a nearby curb and pulled my T-shirt over my knees for warmth. Then I wrapped my arms around my torso.

Tears formed streaks on my cheeks. Life really sucked. I felt sorry for my mom, and I felt sorry for myself. I knew nobody should be treated this way.

I huddled curbside for the longest time; at least, that's what it felt like to me. Only a couple of cars passed by in the middle of the night, but the drivers totally ignored the sight of a half-dressed kid sitting on the edge of a sidewalk, bawling his eyes out.

Then two cops in a black-and-white Los Angeles Police Department cruiser happened to pass by. The cop riding on the passenger side aimed a bright white light at me while the cruiser rolled to a quick stop. They parked. The cop driving the car got out first, hitching up his pants as he made his way toward me.

"What are you doing out here?" the LAPD field officer asked. "Something wrong?"

"My mom got hit by my dad, and my mom told me to run. So I'm out here."

"You know where you live?"

"Sure. Around the corner."

"Can you take us there?"

I led them to the apartment complex on foot. The cops didn't waste any time. They stormed through the front door with the lead cop marching straight to the bedroom, loaded for bear. He flipped on the light, saw streaks of blood on the walls, and my mother curled up in the closet. My startled father, rubbing his eyes, had been sleeping in the bed.

The cop grabbed my father by the arm and dragged him out to the living room—my dad's feet never touching the ground. The next thing my father knew, the cop slammed him against a wall and began raining punches on his body.

"You like hitting women?" the cop asked. "Well, how do you like this?"

A series of punches to the kidneys stifled any sort of response from my father. He yelped in pain from blow after blow.

"You still like hitting women?" the cop continued. "Then you're not going to like this."

Another set of body blows smothered my father's midsection.

More cops and a paramedic unit arrived. My father was handcuffed and pushed onto the couch while emergency personnel tended to my battered mother. They insisted on taking my mother to a nearby hospital, but she would not leave the apartment. They bandaged her up as best as they could and placed her back in bed.

My father was arrested and spent the night in jail. He was released in the morning, and when he walked up the stairway to our apartment, I was stunned.

Shouldn't this guy be sitting in jail?

I don't know why my father was released so quickly. Things were calm for a few days, but then my father returned to his old ways of beating Mom. The assaults weren't as violent, meaning that he stopped short of drawing blood, but I'm sure they hurt all the same.

I knew there was nothing I could do to stop my father, who had received merely a slap on the wrist from the court system.

I just had to wait until I got older to exact justice.

◆　◆　◆

It was around this time that my father started dealing drugs on the street—mainly marijuana and cocaine. I had found baggies of pot in one of his clothes drawers, so I wasn't surprised when Mom told me that he had been arrested for dealing. I didn't mind at all that he got arrested. When that happened, I figured I was guaranteed several days of peace until he was released on bail. But all this turmoil created upheaval. Life really stank. I hated who I was and where I lived.

My grandmother—my mother's mother—came for an extended visit from the old country. I loved my grandma. She was kind to me. She loved to cook a popular El Salvadoran dish called *pupusa*, which was made up of thick corn tortillas filled with anything from meats to cheeses to refried beans and pork rinds.

One time while my *abuela* was making her famous *pupusa*, I found a lighter in the living room. I'd seen lighters before, but I was Curious George that night. I wanted to see if I could start a fire with the lighter. Don't ask me why or what got into me, but that's what I wanted to do.

Something told me it wouldn't be a good idea to light something on fire in the living room, so I tiptoed into my parents' bedroom. Nobody noticed I closed the door. What could I light on fire? I know . . . one of my father's old T-shirts. He'd never miss it. I put the lighter to the T-shirt, and to my great surprise, it burst into flames so quickly that I had to toss it away, in case I burned myself.

The burning T-shirt landed next to the curtains covering the only window. The sheer curtains, made of fading cotton lace, quickly caught fire. I had no idea what to do. I certainly didn't want to tell my mother or grandmother that the curtains were on fire. The only bright spot was that my father wasn't there. He would've *killed* me for setting his curtains on fire.

When flames had engulfed the curtains and became a bigger blaze, I slipped out of the bedroom and closed the door behind me. My mother and grandmother were busy preparing dinner in the kitchen and didn't notice me or smell smoke. I decided to act as nonchalantly as possible. I turned on the TV and plopped myself down on the couch to watch some cartoons.

Out of the corner of my eye, I saw my grandmother leave the

kitchen, wiping her hands on her apron. She had to use the facilities. The bathroom was right next to my parents' bedroom.

She must have sensed something or smelled smoke. Grandma touched the doorknob to the bedroom and immediately recoiled because the handle was so hot.

"Fire! Fire!" she screamed.

Things happened pretty quickly after that. My mother picked up the phone and dialed 911 while my grandmother grabbed me and her purse and hustled me out of the apartment. My mother, as panicked as I had ever seen her, grabbed her belongings and ran out after us.

After descending three flights of stairs among other panicked residents, I looked up at our corner unit. I could see flames licking the windowsill and black smoke rising to the sky. My shock and awe were broken by the sounds of fire engines and sirens splitting the sky.

I don't remember how many apartment units, including ours, burned up that day. It may have been two or three. While the fire crews were mopping up, an important-looking man in a blue uniform asked me if I had seen anything.

"Oh, yeah," I said. "There were some kids playing outside our window. They were messing around with matches."

"Do you remember what kids they were?" asked the investigator.

"No, I never saw them before."

I wasn't bothered after that, although all these years later, I wonder why the fireman believed me. Anyone could tell that the fire started *inside* the unit.

We had to move, of course. I truly don't remember where we lived right after the fire.

I don't like to think about those days.

chapter three

STEALING AWAY

The reason why I don't remember much about where we lived after the fire is because we must have moved to an apartment close to 9th and Kenmore. I do remember moving a couple of times before my parents settled into a two-bedroom apartment at 9th and New Hampshire, three blocks away from my old home.

No matter where we lived, my world didn't extend beyond a few blocks in any direction. I would soon learn, however, that there was a whole different way of growing up just a matter of miles from our neighborhood.

Here's what happened: I was in the third grade at Hoover Elementary when Miss Gardner, my teacher, announced, "Class, I have exciting news. Each one of you is going to have a pen pal."

A pen pal? I had no idea what that meant. Nor was I aware that Miss Gardner had arranged for a third-grade class in a much wealthier part of Los Angeles—Santa Monica—to exchange letters with us.

"You're going to have a great time writing your special pen pal," Miss Gardner said. "It's like having a conversation with a friend, but it's on paper."

"But what are we supposed to write about, Teacher?" one of the kids in my class asked.

"Anything you want," she replied. "That's the great thing about having a pen pal. You can write about anything you choose. You can share your thoughts, your dreams, and even your secrets with your pen pal."

I couldn't think of anything to say. What was I going to tell a complete stranger about myself? I didn't get it.

"Here's a sheet of paper you can write on." Miss Gardner started passing out blank sheets of paper to the class. "Write as much as you want."

Yeah, right.

I knew I had to scribble something, although my cursive was atrocious. At least, that's what Miss Gardner was always telling me. I tapped my pencil on the piece of paper. The best I could come up with was this: "My name is Darwin. How are you?"

Darwin was my legal name. I have no idea why my parents named me after Charles Darwin—the nineteenth-century British naturalist best known for his theory of evolution. Latino parents sometimes love to name their children after a famous personality, but why they chose Darwin was and remains a mystery to me.

No one in the schoolyard called me Darwin, though. Early in my third-grade year, I suddenly decided during recess—on the spur of the moment—that I didn't like my first name anymore.

"I don't want anybody calling me Darwin," I said to a bunch of my classmates. "I want you to call me Casey."

Casey? Where did that name come from?

To this day, I don't know. I pulled the name out of thin air. Nobody in our family was named Casey. Maybe I heard the name mentioned on a TV show. Maybe I had read the baseball poem "Casey at the Bat" in school. All I know is that the name Casey quickly took hold and anyone who knows me—including my parents and close family—calls me Casey.

Within a week of writing my pen pal, I received a nice reply from a boy named Brett. He talked about how he liked to go to the beach. I had never been to the coast, although we lived less than fifteen miles from the Pacific Ocean, so I couldn't imagine what playing in the sand and surf was like. We exchanged letters back and forth throughout the school year, never writing more than a line or two.

In the late spring, Miss Gardner told us she had some exciting news to share. "Class, you're going to get the chance to meet the boy or girl you've been writing to all school year. We're going to go on a field trip to meet your special pen pal, so have one of your parents sign the permission slip."

Miss Gardner walked up and down the class rows, handing each student a field trip form and a sheet of instructions. "Make sure you get your permission slips signed by a parent or guardian. We have some fun activities planned, including flying a kite. Be sure to bring one with you."

I didn't have a kite, and I knew we weren't going to buy one. My parents were broke—although the term *poor* would be more correct. If it was a choice between eating dinner or buying a kite, then we were going to eat dinner.

On the morning of the big field trip, the bus ride to Santa Monica was a revelation. I couldn't see much along the freeway, but once we turned onto the off-ramp, I couldn't believe how green and lush everything was. The manicured bungalows and stately houses were beautiful—well maintained, freshly painted, and inviting. None of them had bars on the windows.

I looked around the bus. Every jaw had dropped. The silence was deafening. Reality hit everyone at the same time: *we had just found out how poor we were.*

The private school was surrounded by belts of green grass and dotted with towering palm trees. We were led off the bus to a main hallway inside the school. The linoleum floor glistened. No trash anywhere. Tidy lockers.

We were escorted into a third-grade classroom to meet our pen pals. Dressed in crisp uniforms—white, button-down dress shirts and beige pants for the boys and plaid skirts for the girls—the preppy students were standing to greet us. All the kids were white. I didn't see one Latino or black student.

Their teacher called for attention. "Class, it's time for you to meet your pen pals," she announced. Names were called, and I was introduced to Brett. He had wavy brown hair and seemed nice enough. We were given a couple of projects to do and then escorted to the cafeteria, where a hot lunch was waiting for us. We were fed all the pizza we wanted, which was cool.

After lunch, the students were told to fetch their kites and meet in the playground behind the school. I was the only student without a kite. Once again, I felt left out. My family couldn't afford a kite, which left me feeling bummed.

I hurried out to the playground, hoping no one would notice that I didn't have a kite in my hand. The acre of green grass took my breath away. The vividness of the emerald green lawn, ringed by the mature trees, dense vegetation, and large homes beyond the perimeter of the playground, was astonishing.

"Where's your kite?"

I turned around. Brett was holding a kite and a ball of string in his hands.

"I forgot mine." I hoped that he would believe my lame excuse.

"Then you can help me fly mine," he said.

I didn't see how that was possible, but I mumbled thanks anyway.

The teachers directed the students to spread out and stand in a line to launch our kites all at the same time. "On the count of three, everyone run together," said Brett's teacher. "Remember, hold your kite above your head so the wind can catch it."

The students fanned out from one end of the field to the other. With arms raised, Brett's teacher began the countdown.

"Three . . . two . . . one. *Run!*"

Every kid started sprinting, holding their kites aloft. I didn't make a move. I couldn't. I didn't have a kite. It was obvious to me as well as everyone else that I didn't belong on that grassy field. I watched as more than fifty kids attempted to get their kites up in the air.

None of the teachers noticed that I was the only one left behind. Not one person made a move toward me; it was like I was invisible.

Only a few successfully launched their kites, so for the next half hour, kids kept trying to get their kites aloft using the westerly breezes. I moped around the field, counting the minutes until our departure back to the inner city. As far as I was concerned, we couldn't leave Santa Monica fast enough. When I got on the bus, I made sure I got a window seat so I didn't have to talk to anybody.

As we motored out of the parking lot and onto the surface streets of a well-kept, wealthy neighborhood, I became lost in thoughts of isolation. If I needed any confirmation that my life really sucked, this was it.

✦ ✦ ✦

Third grade wasn't a total loss.

That's because Mike Rodriguez became my best friend. He was the only white kid in an elementary school that was probably 60 percent Latino and 40 percent black.

Actually, Mike wasn't Caucasian. He just looked white because of his fair skin and blond hair. Even though he appeared to be "full white," his dad was Mexican American, but I didn't care about that. Like my father, his dad was never around, which is another reason we gravitated toward each other. But Mike's dad had a good excuse for not being in the picture: he was in prison.

Without male tethers in our lives, we naturally fell in with each other. Our bond deepened when we started stealing stuff together. Shoplifting. Snatching items off shelves. Jacking anything that wasn't nailed down.

I didn't think it was wrong to steal. I easily justified my behavior. Since I didn't have anything—which wasn't fair—how could stealing be bad?

Mike and I started with shoplifting snacks and drinks from a nearby 7-Eleven and liquor stores in the neighborhood. We'd put bags of potato chips and cans of soda pop inside our backpacks in the back of the store—at a time before surveillance cameras were widespread. Then we'd go to the front and buy a pack of Wrigley gum so the clerk didn't get suspicious of our presence inside the store. We were surprised how our scam always worked.

One time, Miss Gardner told us to bring snacks for a class party just before spring break. Mike and I agreed that a bag of Lay's Potato Chips and a can of A&W root beer wouldn't do it. Before school one morning, we scoped out the local 7-Eleven and waited until a bunch of customers walked in to buy their morning coffee and doughnuts, which would keep the clerk busy at the cash register.

We snuck inside and eased our way to the back of the snack aisle, wearing our school backpacks. Mike knelt down, and I opened his backpack and stuffed it with small bags of Fritos, tortilla chips, and corn nuts. I added a few candy bars for good measure. Then it was my turn to kneel while Mike opened my backpack and filled it with loot.

This time we didn't bother buying a pack of gum. We slithered past the line of customers and hustled outside. As soon as we were out of sight, Mike and I cracked up, laughing at how good we were as a team of thieves.

When we arrived at Hoover Elementary, we opened up our

bulging backpacks, and man, we were the guys. Our classmates must have thought, *Their parents must be well off. Look at all that stuff!*

Mike and I kept our mouths shut. We weren't about to blab about where we got our snacks and goodies.

◆ ◆ ◆

What was life like when we weren't in school?

Keep in mind that my neighborhood of 9th and New Hampshire was my reality in my elementary school years, so that's all I knew.

There weren't any parks nearby, so we played baseball in the streets and touch football in vacant lots. The rest of the time we hung out with friends and talked, swapped funny stories, and generally messed around like the little kids we were. When we got bored or hungry, we'd go steal something to eat at a convenience store. I still can't believe everything we got away with.

Just as there was violence in my home, there was an undercurrent of violence on the streets. I was still in third grade when I witnessed my first kidnapping. Mike and I were walking down the street late one afternoon when we heard a Chevy sedan slam on its brakes half a block behind us. A black guy hopped out and ran toward a Korean schoolgirl walking by herself. She looked a couple of years older than us.

Everything happened so fast: in one fell swoop, he grabbed and swept her into the driver's side of the front seat. A brutal shove kept her down. Then the Chevy roared to life with the black guy behind the wheel. As he passed by, he made eye contact with me.

I involuntarily shivered. For a fleeting second, I thought he was going to slam on his brakes and grab me, but he kept on driving.

And that was it. I never found out what happened to the little girl.

A month or two later, I was hanging around the 7-Eleven when another black guy in a similar-looking Chevy four-door sedan screeched to a halt across the street. He got out and seized a boy who looked to be in junior high. I was mesmerized by a replay of what I had witnessed earlier: a screeching car, a snatched child, and a quick getaway.

Although my young mind couldn't understand why this was happening or what the fate was of these kids on the street, I knew it was scary. *Should I say anything to my parents or my teacher?*

I dismissed the thought. My father wouldn't care, my mother wouldn't know what to do, and it was too risky mentioning something to my teacher.

◆　◆　◆

A couple of months later, I was hanging out in the back of our apartment building, on the third floor. I sat on the metal fire escape stairway that overlooked an alleyway, allowing my legs to dangle in the late-afternoon sun after school.

I saw three guys, all Latinos, walking through the alley. Nothing unusual about that. They wore tight jeans and black leather jackets, typical dress for the MS-13—Mara Salvatrucha—gang members at the time. With their long hair and heavy metal stoner look, they sure appeared to be tough guys.

A black Toyota Camry—with custom rims and wide tires— pulled into the alley and crept past them. Then the four-door sedan turned into our apartment carport and took an empty parking space.

The driver stepped out of the car and walked toward the three men. Suddenly, the guy reached into his waistband and pulled out a handgun. He raised his right arm and started firing.

Blam, blam . . . blam, blam.

The first two men slumped and fell to the ground, holding their stomachs. Actually, one screamed when he got hit—a blood-curdling scream. But his shrieks were short-lived. He went mute within seconds, and both bodies lay perfectly still. Something told me they were dead.

All this happened in an instant.

From my third-story perch, I watched the double murder unfold. For some reason I didn't freeze, nor did I flinch when the rounds of bullets went off. Although I was out in the open, I didn't think about hightailing it for safety. Instead, I was transfixed at what I was witnessing—like watching an action movie.

The third man knew he was next. He looked left and right for cover—and darted for the carport underneath me. The assassin quickly reloaded his handgun and raised his weapon to fire.

I overheard the man pleading for his life. "Don't kill me! Mom! Mom, I need you!"

There was no mercy. The shooter fired off two shots, and the pleading stopped.

The assassin never looked in my direction as he put his gun back into his waistband and walked quickly to his car. His steps were sure and confident. The Camry started up, and he was gone.

How did observing a gangland execution when I was so young impact me? I think the biggest lesson I learned was that life is cheap and could end at any time.

◆　　◆　　◆

So this was my environment as I entered fourth grade and turned ten years old. I was witnessing gang activity, kidnappings, and killings. Cars chasing cars with loud music blaring. Gang members hanging out on street corners, smoking cigarettes or puffing on a joint and passing it on to the next guy.

And then there was the graffiti that proliferated like wild ivy on a wall. Gang members used graffiti to mark their territory or turf or to declare their allegiance to the gang. Gang members from MS-13, 18th Street, and the Rockwood Street Locos would cross out each other's tags and write their own name, which was an indication that another feud could turn deadly. If there was a down arrow next to a gang name painted in a different color, something was going to happen.

My best buddy Mike and I liked hanging out with Randy Arroyo, who was our age. Randy had a brother five years older than me named Pedro. He was in high school and naturally, a ten-year-old kid is going to look up to a fifteen-year-old teetering on the ledge between kid and young adult.

Pedro noticed that I was interested in what he did—or who he was becoming. Or maybe he sensed the hole in my heart from not having the security of a father who loved me. Or maybe he liked being asked questions about what it was like being part of a gang.

One night, we were over at the Sanchez house. No parents were around, so we could say whatever we wanted. "What's this gang stuff all about?" I asked. "How does it work?"

Pedro shot up out of the couch. A smile creased his face as he paced the living room. "It's cool, man. We stick together, and it's like a family. We protect each other. We have parties, and there are girls. It's all good."

"How do you join?" I asked.

"You get jumped in."

"Jumped in? What's that?"

"Well, we choose a few guys to jump you. You know—kick you, sock you around a bit—to see if you can take it. We count to thirteen and then we stop. If you can go the distance, you're in."

Thirteen seconds? That didn't sound too long. How much could it hurt if people kick you for thirteen seconds?

Pedro was my hero. Even though he was too young to have a driver's license, I watched him drive around in nice cars—cars that everyone knew were stolen—like he was a conqueror. He and his buddies were always laughing, appearing not to have a care in the world. I imagined him being part of some amazing adventures as a gang member.

✦ ✦ ✦

When I turned eleven, I knew I wanted to be part of something bigger than myself. I wanted to be accepted, to be told that I belonged. Those really were my feelings as a fifth-grader.

I'll never forget the day I asked Pedro if I could jump in to his gang, which was called the Rockwood Street Locos, one of the hundreds of gangs in South-Central Los Angeles.

"You're a little young," he said. "I'll have to get back to you."

I didn't know about the unwritten age "requirements" at the time—that gangs like their new members to be fifteen or sixteen years old, although they did take in kids as young as twelve because when they got arrested and sent to Juvenile Hall, they were released quickly and back on the streets. All I knew was that I wanted to have what Pedro had—a family that protected him and cared for him.

The next day Pedro drove up in a nice car while I was hanging out on a street corner. The passenger side window rolled down, and Pedro leaned over to have a word.

"Hey, Casey. Good news. You're in. Hop in."

That's all I needed to hear. I was taken to a random house, where a trio of Rockwood members were waiting—Rabbit, Shadow, and Bunny. The next thing I knew, I was thrown to the ground and four guys started stomping on me. A couple of them punched me in my shoulders and neck. I closed my eyes, grimaced, and told myself not to say anything as I got pummeled. And then just as quickly as it started, the beating stopped.

"You okay?" Rabbit was the first to extend a hand to lift me off the floor.

I knew I was going to be black and blue in a few places in the morning, but I wasn't about to admit weakness.

"Sure. I'm okay," I managed.

Stern looks turned to smiles, soul-brother handshakes, and hugs.

I had passed an important rite of passage. This was the first inkling of camaraderie I had ever felt—a sense that I belonged to something greater than myself. They wouldn't have asked me to join Rockwood Street if they didn't *want* me to be part of their gang.

But I would also learn that was just the beginning. I would have to pass another initiation test far different—and more difficult—than getting beat up for thirteen seconds.

✦ ✦ ✦

Rabbit took me under his wing and became my mentor to gang life.

There was a lot I had to learn, which came through tagging along with Rabbit, who became like a big brother to me. He was sixteen, a year older than Pedro, but much wiser in the ways of the streets. I quickly discovered that he was one of the most popular guys in Rockwood—and would later learn that he was one of the most violent.

First, there were the parties where I was introduced to drinking alcohol and took my first hits of marijuana. Keep in mind that I was still eleven years old, so I was incredibly young. At that "tweener" age, I was done with being a kid. I wanted to be a teenager and act like a teenager.

I stayed up late and drove around a lot and tagged mason-stone walls with large *R*s and *W*s—Rockwood's gang symbols. Then we stole a few cars, a process that taught me the rudiments of hot-wiring an automobile. All in all, typical gangbanging stuff.

One evening, Rabbit asked me to join him on a nighttime outing. I had no problem saying yes. He was the boss.

Rabbit picked me up in a stolen Toyota. We drove for a while and entered an unfamiliar part of downtown LA.

"This is 18th Street turf," Rabbit said as storefronts and apartment buildings flashed by.

Rabbit schooled me on the lay of the land. In this part of LA,

18th Street contended for territory with MS-13, Avenues, Harpys Dead End, Easy Riders, and Rockwood, to name a few of the more prominent gangs in my part of downtown Los Angeles.

"If an 18th Street gang leader tells you to do something, or if you don't show proper respect to another gang member, for sure you're beaten by the rest of the gang," Rabbit said. "They kill habitual offenders execution style."

Eighteenth Street gangbangers were easy to identify, he added. Many wore Lakers and Dodgers jerseys with the number 18 on the back. Symbols like XV3, XVIII, and X8 were also used.

Rabbit suddenly turned into an alley like he knew where he was going. Then he gunned the engine and raced through the alley at a high clip, gripping the steering wheel tighter as we drove deeper into 18th Street territory. The speed we were traveling at scared me. I thought we might crash at any moment or another car would back out and cause a nasty wreck. (Of course, I wasn't wearing a seatbelt—that was for sissies.)

"There's a score to settle," he said ominously.

I gulped. My heart was already pumping at double rate because I thought we would surely crash and I would die.

"A dude named Pedro. He doesn't know what's coming," Rabbit said.

Eventually, we slowed down . . . and cruised a couple of alleys. That's when Rabbit spotted his mark.

"That's him."

I noticed a tall figure walking ahead of us. How Rabbit knew that was the person he was looking for, I didn't know, but he was sure he had found him.

We pulled over. In a flash, Rabbit rushed him. I was on his heels. We had the element of surprise on our side.

Rabbit tackled him to the ground, then quickly got to his feet first and aimed a kick to Pedro's abdomen. The blow found one of his kidneys, which prompted a scream.

Rabbit waved his arm. It was my turn. I gave Pedro my swiftest kick to his back. Then Rabbit leaned over and punched him in the head. I followed suit. Several blows rendered Pedro mute. He curled up in a ball, hands over his head to protect himself.

"That's for Rockwood!" Rabbit screamed. "You're never going to mess with the Locos again!"

I took up the chant as well. "Yeah, that's for Rockwood!" I yelled in a high-pitched voice since I had yet to start puberty.

We rained blow after blow upon the gang member, who was crying and begging for mercy.

Then Rabbit reached into his back pocket for a screwdriver—a typical flat-blade hand tool made of tough steel to resist bending.

What I witnessed next is something I will never forget. Rabbit thrust the screwdriver into the soft midsection of the beaten-down gang member. Not once or twice . . . but three times.

Witnessing this violence didn't bother me that much. I knew enough about gangbanging and that gang members got snuffed all the time. We had lost a few in our ranks already. I felt no mercy for Pedro, who writhed in agony. He wasn't dead, but he certainly wasn't going anywhere.

Rabbit looked at me. Once we made eye contact, he tossed me the screwdriver.

"You try it," he said.

I hesitated for a moment. After all, I was eleven years old.

"What are you waiting for?" Rabbit asked. "Just do it."

A shot of adrenaline swept through my veins. Retightening my grip on the screwdriver, I leaned over and let him have it in his back. But the screwdriver didn't pierce his skin.

"Try again. This time in his stomach. Just do it harder," Rabbit coached. "Go right into him."

With all the strength I could summon, I plunged the screwdriver into his soft underbelly. Sure enough, the blade entered into his gut like a knife into a stick of butter. I pushed until the shaft was halfway inside his body. The screwdriver didn't go all the way in, but I knew it was inside his guts because I felt a weird vibration in my hand.

And then I pulled out the screwdriver, covered in blood and white junk.

"Let's jam," Rabbit said.

We left the Hoover gang member bleeding in the street.

I don't know if he lived or not. Frankly, I didn't care. The important thing is that I had done what Rabbit asked.

"You have a future with us." Rabbit had a satisfied look as he veered into the night traffic.

That was all he had to say to receive my complete allegiance to him and Rockwood.

chapter four

NO RANKING OUT

When people hear about young boys and young men being part of a *gang*, they have an image of similarly dressed gangbangers participating in home invasions, taking part in carjackings, and settling scores in violent ways. That image, I would learn quickly, was close to reality. It didn't take me long to figure out that the streets were bloody. Most of the time it was kill or be killed.

What many people don't know about street gangs is that sometimes gangs are quite friendly with each other, especially when it's in everyone's best interest to get along. Friendly gangs share turf, meaning they divvy up the drug trade. Another reason some gangs get along is because of family members. Brothers, uncles, or cousins often belong to different gangs, so blood ties cut across lines of demarcation.

Sometimes in the neighborhood, you're challenged to declare your allegiance. You can't "rank out," meaning you can't equivocate when asked if you belong to a particular gang or not. You have to be "all in" with your gang if that happens. That's what I was taught.

One time, when I was twelve years old, Shady and I were riding our Sting-Ray bikes—the ones with big handlebars and "banana" seats—in the neighborhood. We had stopped at the corner of Vermont and Pico when Shady spotted a trio of Easy Riders, part of a Latino street gang, pedaling their Sting-Rays toward us. Shady took off without a word, bolting down the hill. I had no idea why he was going southbound on Vermont with three Easy Riders in pursuit, so I followed.

It was a long chase—a good mile. I hadn't caught up with them when Shady pulled into the parking lot of a small neighborhood market. He threw his bike to the side and sprinted into the store—presumably for safety since the Easy Riders weren't far behind. When they arrived, they tossed their String-Rays aside and ran into the store after Shady.

I raced to the store entrance and jammed on the pedal brakes, laying down a long skid. I hopped off my bike and wondered what I would find inside.

I found the three Easy Riders in a stand-off with Shady next to the candy aisle. Shady's pursuers looked to be several years older but weren't quite old enough to drive. As for me, I was a five-foot scrub who weighed maybe ninety pounds soaking wet.

The tallest of the three, acting tough, grabbed Shady's ball cap and twirled it in his hand. "I know you're from Rockwood," he said. Then he noticed me. "You're from Rockwood too, shrimp," he sneered.

Shady and I were attired in the usual Rockwood garb: gray hoodies and oversized Levi's 501s that were pleated and cuffed. On the bottom of my pants legs, I had made a one-inch-long slit so that the pants "flared" over my blue Nike Cortez sneakers. At the time, Nike Cortez shoes were so popular among local gangs that LAPD detectives asked Nike to stop selling them because every homicide investigation showed Nike Cortez footprints leaving the crime scene.

Shady raised his arms in mock surrender. "You've got the wrong dudes," he said. "We're not with Rockwood."

I couldn't believe it. Shady ranked out right in front of me.

The tallest kid turned to me. "What about you? Where are you from?" He was clearly testing my loyalty.

I didn't hesitate. Sticking out my jaw and speaking with an attitude, I answered, "Rockwood." I claimed my neighborhood, although I knew that declaring my allegiance meant I could get stomped on, even inside a convenience store.

The tall kid nodded, approvingly. "This dude has heart," he announced to his buddy. Then he looked at Shady. "You're a punk," he said.

And just like that, the confrontation was over. "Let's jam," he said to his fellow gang member, giving us a pass.

When they were gone, I looked at Shady. "Why did you rank out, man?"

"I dunno." Shady shrugged his shoulders. Looking back, he was clearly scared of getting beaten up, but he had broken an unwritten rule.

That rule says you stand up for your gang. I learned that from Rabbit, who mentored me about gang life. One time Rabbit and I were hanging out together when we ran into three guys from MS-13 at a street corner. They stopped us, and once again, the first question we heard was this: "Are you from Rockwood?"

Rabbit stood his ground. "Yeah, I'm with Rockwood," he said, knowing that he could be putting his life on the line for saying so. Fortunately for him, no altercation ensued, and everyone stayed cool that night, but I idolized him for his courage.

✦ ✦ ✦

I loved roaming the neighborhood with Rabbit. I didn't know it at the time, but I was seeking male approval. I wanted to hear that I was good enough, that I belonged. Since Rabbit was one of those guys I looked up to, I wanted to show him that I could be counted on to do anything he asked me to—from stealing cars to swiping bikes, sneakers, or skateboards at his command. If he needed me to bust out the window of a parked car to snatch a backpack or rummage through a glove compartment, I was his guy.

The Rockwood gang members spoke English to each other. Things are different today because many Latino gang members don't know how to speak English very well, but back in my era, everyone spoke English. In fact, if you spoke Spanish, you were made fun of—like you were uneducated. We were in America, right?

The MS-13 guys, however, recruited refugees mainly from the "Northern Triangle"—Guatemala, El Salvador, and Honduras. Since they hadn't been in this country long enough to assimilate and pick up English, they spoke Spanish to each other. The language barrier between us made it easy for our two gangs to generate a genuine dislike for each other.

On top of that, the MS-13 guys in our neighborhood were hotheads and looking to make a name for themselves. One time I was with Randy Arroyo and his older brother, Pedro, who jumped me into Rockwood. We were hanging out and wasting time in an abandoned building, during the middle of the day, when Pedro showed me a palm-sized silver gun he had recently acquired. I was admiring the craftsmanship when we heard voices. Suddenly, ten members of MS-13 stepped inside an open door. It was on.

Outnumbered, Pedro directed us to retreat behind a couple of empty barrels.

Taunts were exchanged from a distance, the most common being, "Let's get down to business" from the leader of this MS-13 clique.

Cliques are smaller gangs within a gang. Many cliques operate independently and autonomously in gang neighborhoods.

I was still in sixth grade at the time—and just as impulsive as anyone else. I thought if I could get Pedro's gun, I could take out these MS-13 guys.

"Pedro, just let me have your piece. I can get two dudes right now."

"Forget it," he replied. "I'll take care of this."

"Give me this chance, man. I can take these dudes down."

I had no problem following through on my bravado. In my heart, I knew I could pull the trigger and take another person's life. I was ready to commit murder.

"No, I got this." Pedro was firm.

Suddenly, the standoff ended when the MS-13 guys spun on their heels and left the building. I had no idea why the confrontation ended that way, but part of me was disappointed. I wanted to shoot one or two guys. The possibility of committing an act of violence excited me.

I've thought long and hard about why I felt that way when I was so young. I've already described how I grew up watching my father beat my mother—hitting her full force in the face with his fists, throwing her to the ground, and kicking her time after time as she crawled into a ball and whimpered, unable to resist his blows. He beat her like a man would beat another man. Witnessing the thrashings built up a lot of rage inside of me. I needed an outlet to release the bottled-up feelings of fury and anger I felt for my father.

I hated him for the way he treated Mom and cuffed me behind the ears when he was drunk, which happened nearly every day. I'm not exaggerating when I say there was never a two-day period when he wasn't intoxicated, or when he wasn't screaming at my mother and me, or when he wasn't slapping and punching the both of us. I believe the main reason why gangs were so attractive is because things were so bad at home. With gangs, I got a chance to have a new family. The streets held an allure for me because I didn't like being in the apartment when my father was around.

◆   ◆   ◆

There was another reason I didn't like hanging around our home: rats had the run of the apartment. They were everywhere, like the time I came home and found my mom passed out from another beating. I happened to open a closet door and saw a big fat rat staring at me, surrounded by a litter of pink baby rats. I closed that door really quick. As I grew older, I developed a phobia about rats and hated seeing them run around the apartment, scurrying for cover whenever I discovered them.

Besides rodents that behaved fearlessly, there were two other significant childhood events that shaped my psyche—my human mind, soul, and spirit.

The first happened when I was an infant in El Salvador. I don't remember this event since I was so young, but my mother told me this story several times while I was growing up.

We were living with my great-grandmother at the time, who was getting up there in age. Inside my great-grandmother's kitchen were small glass containers used to store various liquids. Don't ask me how or why, but one of those containers contained gasoline.

One evening, my great-grandmother reached for a small glass jar that contained apple juice to pour into my nighttime bottle. Instead of grabbing the apple juice, however, she took the glass jar containing gasoline.

I was put down in my crib, and the bottle was angled in such a way that I could easily grab it and drink. That's what I sipped on that night.

Sometime later, my mom and great-grandmother dropped by my room to check on me—and the pungent smell of gasoline horrified them. Mom screamed and checked the bottle. I had consumed the gasoline, and the bottle was nearly empty.

She held me up and looked at me. The color of my face was totally drained, and my eyes rolled back in their sockets.

Panic grabbed my mother by the throat. She tried to force me to vomit but had no luck, so she and my great-grandmother rushed me to the local hospital. I'm not sure what the emergency room doctors did to save my life, but I somehow survived the harrowing experience.

I have often wondered what that incident did to my developing brain and how much damage drinking gasoline did to my major organs. Besides causing irritation of the gastric tract and creating breathing difficulties, consuming gasoline carries major health implications—similar to what those sniffing glue or intoxicating inhalants experience: disorientation, hallucinations, and disassociation with the environment. What did consuming gasoline as an infant do to the "hard-wiring" of my brain?

I'm sure it did something.

◆　◆　◆

During my first year of gang life, I learned that MS-13 weren't our main rivals, not by a long shot. We had to contend with cliques like Big Top, Diamond Street, Temple Street, and The Rascals.

When we weren't getting ready to rumble, my homies and I were conducting acts of larceny—home invasions, car break-ins, convenience store shoplifting, and the like.

Since I was stealing so much, it wasn't long before I got arrested for breaking-and-entering a car. I was twelve years old.

I was loaded into a cop car with hands cuffed behind my back—that was a first-time experience—and driven to Rampart Station, the LAPD's police station serving communities west of downtown Los Angeles. Everything was a blur, but after being processed, I was bused to Central Juvenile Hall in Boyle Heights.

I had a lot of time to think about what being locked up would be like. I had heard stories from my homies about how you have to be tough and show that you're not going to take crap from anyone. I fixed it in my mind that nobody was going to do anything stupid with me. If that happened, then I could go off on him, right?

That's how my twelve-year-old mind was working.

I got off the bus and was led to a reception area, where a deputy directed me to sit on a bench that was bolted to the floor. My cuffs were taken off. Another kid my age was sitting on the other end of the bench.

We looked at each other. "Where are you from?" he asked.

He was friendly. He didn't grunt *Where are you from?* in a harsh way at all. The question was asked genuinely.

He didn't know that I had vowed to myself that the first guy who said anything to me was going to feel my fists. In a flash I took the first swing. The next thing I remember is fighting and wrestling each other to the floor. I didn't know what gang he was from or who he was. He was simply in the wrong place at the wrong time.

A black counselor broke into the reception area from a side door. This guy was as huge as an NFL lineman.

He grabbed me by the scruff of the neck and heaved me against a mint-colored wall. I bounced off the concrete wall like a sack of potatoes. *Man, that hurt.* The next thing I knew, I was handcuffed and dragged out of the reception area and taken to my intake housing unit. I was processed into a unit of approximately two or three dozen other boys who were assigned one- and two-person sleeping rooms.

Everything was different: the food, getting undressed in front of everybody in the showers, and always asking permission before moving around the unit. I didn't like the rules, especially the one where I had to walk with my hands behind my back or not look into anyone else's room.

I found out that the kid I tussled with in the reception area was part of MS-13. I had a rule for anyone associated with MS-13: they weren't going to be my friends. If I got into fights that kept me quarantined to my sleeping room for a couple of days, then that was an acceptable trade-off for me.

One guy from MS-13 got under my skin. I didn't like his face, so I decided to do something about it. Inside the classroom, I sharpened my pencil at the sharpener attached to the wall. I made sure the point was as sharp as could be.

Then I walked past the desk belonging to the MS-13 gang member. He didn't notice me, but I certainly observed that his right hand was lying flat on the desk. At exactly the right moment, I grabbed his wrist with my left hand and plunged the pencil point into his hand—pressing the pencil to the hilt as he screamed to the heavens.

Satisfied that I had inflicted intense pain, I removed the pencil, which was dripping with blood. The gang member, turning white from shock, looked at his bleeding hand that was shaking from the trauma.

The entire classroom freaked out. The teacher momentarily didn't know what to do. She quickly gathered her wits and pressed the panic button under her desktop. Juvie counselors and guards swarmed inside the classroom and grabbed me, roughing me up in the process. But I didn't care. As they hauled me away, I laughed. That was one more MS-13 member who wasn't going to bother me or any of my homies ever again.

I was cuffed and led to a room where a staff psychologist was waiting for me. We talked for a while; about what, I can't remember. Talking about my feelings or why I did things wasn't important to me.

I was put into solitary confinement inside a tiny room that was away from the other juvenile population. I lost all my rights as far as going outside my cell or mingling with other juvenile delinquents.

This was a pivotal moment in my life. After going off like that, I was given a label that stuck to me like black roofing tar: I was a rules-don't-apply-to-me type of guy and a nut ball who could turn crazy on anybody at any time. I can assure you that everyone knew who Casey Diaz was after word got around about the pencil stabbing.

I was allowed to rejoin the juvenile population after a week or so and released not long after that. Juvenile Hall became a revolving door: I'd be out for a few weeks, get arrested for some type of gang activity, get hauled off to Juvenile Hall, and then be released in a few days. In and out, in and out. I don't think the authorities knew what to do with me.

◆　◆　◆

I know I put my mom through a lot because it was evident to everyone that I was a delinquent. She had lost control of me. Neither of my parents knew what to say. Mom had her own issues to deal with, like working extra shifts sewing clothes so she could earn enough to keep the rent paid and food on the table.

When I was released from Juvenile Hall and under their roof again, mayhem ruled our home because I was so out of control. I stayed out as late as I wanted with older kids who were obviously up to no good. When it was evident to my mom that gang life was *my* life, she became depressed. My father? I don't think he cared. His biggest concern was drinking enough to get drunk.

One thing about our apartment was that there were always books lying around. That might sound surprising, given what I've shared about my life so far, but my father constantly stressed the importance of reading. If he'd come into the apartment while I was watching a baseball game on TV, he'd snarl and say, "Stupid people watch sports. Sports are for stupid people."

His thing was World War II history books, biographies on figures like Joseph Stalin and Winston Churchill, and books on science and evolution. "If you want to be somebody, then read books," he said, reaching for a hardback on D-Day and flipping it in my direction. "That's for smart people."

Too bad I didn't listen to his advice. I never applied myself to studying or doing my schoolwork; I was into gangbanging—100 percent all the way.

And I hadn't even gone through puberty.

chapter five

GANG PROMOTION

After graduating from Hoover Elementary, I moved on to Berendo Junior High in Central LA for the seventh grade, but I didn't last long because I got kicked out for fighting. I was shipped off to Virgil Junior High, where I got kicked out for getting into another fight with a gang member. That earned me a one-way transfer to Mount Vernon Junior High, and this time it stuck because Mount Vernon was a "neutral" school—no single gang dominated. Everything about the gang scene at Mount Vernon was mellower. I actually became friendly with some of the Drifters, including a girl gang member named Camila.

But there was a gang member whom I didn't click with—a dude from the Harpys. Midway through the school year, we took the measure of each other. I could tell that we'd have it out some day.

One morning toward the end of the academic year, I slipped a folding knife into my front pocket when I left for school. This was a proactive move on my part; I wasn't going to wait for him to stick a sharp blade in my back. I stalked him between classes until I thought it was the right time, and then I stabbed him in the hallway. Not once but two times.

In the predictable chaos that ensued, I slipped away unnoticed.

For only so long. That night, two LAPD cops came by the apartment and busted me, resulting in another trip to Juvenile Hall. I wasn't particularly bothered by this; I felt comfortable at juvie because I'd been locked up there before on many occasions. I always got released within days.

✦ ✦ ✦

In the streets, I was getting a reputation as someone not to mess with. While I thrived from the recognition and respect I received from my homies, I also basked in the knowledge that others were fearful of me. I enjoyed seeing the fright in their eyes and felt powerful when I sensed hesitancy or anxiousness on their part. With each stabbing, stolen car, or robbery, I felt like my future was coming into higher definition as part of the Rockwood gang. I felt like I was growing into a leadership role. That seemed like the direction I was going in life.

I wasn't worried at all about making the jump to high school at the age of fourteen. Sure, the juniors and seniors at Belmont High were bigger and physically more mature than me, but I was wise beyond my years to the ways of the gang world. It helped that Belmont High was dominated by Rockwood, although an 18th Street clique known as the Columbia Lil Cycos also maintained a big presence on campus. Still, Rockwood had the upper hand, and the Lil Cycos knew that. In every classroom, we had somebody from our gang—from our neighborhood—keeping tabs on what was going down in that school.

I'll admit that I had a chip on my shoulder regarding the Columbia Lil Cycos. Why? Because they were an 18th Street clique. Occasionally bad blood spilled over, like the time when I was in class and one of the Lil Cycos' girlfriends noticed that I kept looking over to her boyfriend, a dude named Cricket, like I was measuring him up. Actually, that's exactly what I was doing: I was checking out Cricket and filing away that information for another time.

"What's your problem?" she asked in a raised voice—loud enough for the class lesson to stop and for all eyes to turn in our direction.

Her boyfriend figured out what was going on too. "Yeah, you got a problem?" he chimed in.

"I sure do," I replied. "I don't like you, and I don't like your neighborhood."

The gang member kept his cool, but his girlfriend rose to his defense—literally. She jumped out of her seat and approached my desk, where she stood her ground. I smirked and acted like her antics amused me, but I felt more respect for this girl than for the guy from Lil Cycos because he didn't man up. That didn't mean I was going to let down my guard with Cricket, however. Something about him rubbed me the wrong way, which wasn't unusual in those days. It didn't take much to get on my bad side.

During lunch period, when the Rockwood homies hung out on one side of the cafeteria and Lil Cycos took the other section, I told my guys about the run-in with Cricket and his girlfriend. They all agreed he needed to learn a lesson and I was the perfect person to deliver it.

"Sometime soon, I'm going to take out that Cricket dude," I declared.

✦   ✦   ✦

The school bell rang, signaling lunch was over. I walked out of the cafeteria, still stewing over Cricket and wondering what I should do to set matters right. Suddenly, another guy from Lil Cycos bumped into me for no apparent reason.

He must have heard about my clash with Cricket in the classroom.

He was clearly disrespecting me—and sending a signal that his homie Cricket wasn't to be trifled with. Since I was surrounded by my guys, I couldn't let a challenge like that go unanswered. In an instant, I started booming on him—*whack, whack, whack*. He hit the deck. Students scattered when it became apparent that a gang rumble had commenced.

I was still swinging away when one of my guys told me that school security was on the way. I got out of there as quickly as possible, but not before giving Cricket one more swift kick to the head so that he'd have something to remember me by. Then I slipped away without getting caught.

That afternoon, after my last class, I was hanging out at the school entrance, watching cars come and go when something caught my eye. I noticed a Lil Cycos gang member pushing a Rockwood dude and forcing him to hand over a can of black spray paint.

Everyone knows gangs spray-paint graffiti to mark their territory, but having another gang member demand that you hand over your bottle of spray paint is a major form of disrespect. What bothered me was that our guy didn't do anything about it. His name was Javier.

I chased him down. "What's going on, man?" I asked. "You just let him walk away with our spray can."

A pained look crossed Javier's face. "Sorry, dude. I didn't want to cause trouble."

Hearing his response got me mad—real mad. As much as I wanted to dog my homie for letting the disrespect happen, my hatred for 18th Street and their cliques rose several notches because they were always pulling stunts like this. I had so many disputes with them over the years, so I had to do something or go crazy. A spirit of loathing oozed out of me.

I told my guys, "Let's shank up and teach them a lesson."

Miguel, one of my guys, looked at me. "You can't do that, man. You're going to start a war."

"Join me on this one," I urged.

Miguel needed a bit more convincing, but eventually he and a couple of other guys agreed to have my back as long as I led the way.

I noticed that the 18th Street dude had stopped at an ice cream truck parked outside the school. This was our chance to confront him.

"C'mon, guys," I said. We hustled and caught up with him as he was walking away from the ice cream truck, licking a vanilla cone in one hand and holding the spray can in the other.

"Hey, that's ours," I said without preamble.

"Huh?"

"The spray can. I want it back. This is Rockwood's neighborhood."

The 18th Street gang member shot me a puzzled look. Maybe his English wasn't that good.

I wasn't in the mood to wait for a response. I flipped the switch—and went ballistic crazy. I stabbed him in the face, neck, back, and stomach with many thrusts. He fell to the sidewalk screaming and clutching his wounds. Then I kicked him in the head and left him there, not bothered at all by what I had done or that other schoolkids were running in the opposite direction.

His homeboys got wind of the stabbing—which he survived—and in the tit-for-tat world of gang life, they had to respond or lose face.

Aware that retaliation was heading my way, I decided to hang out at The Hill, a neighborhood near 5th and Union in downtown LA. I figured the 18th Street guys would outnumber us if they showed up, but I didn't care.

As predicted, they came looking for me. It was turning dark when a beat-up Impala full of 18th Street dudes parked at the bottom of The Hill. Some of our guys scattered, but six or seven homies stayed by my side. Since I expected trouble, I made sure I had my hands on a shotgun.

We scoped out the low-riding Chevy from a house above them, so we had the high ground.

Several of them stepped out of the car. "Hey, we want to talk to Casey," one shouted.

"I ain't talking," I yelled back.

"We just want to talk," the 18th Street guy repeated.

From my perch, I could feel their wariness.

"If you come up, I'm going to blast you. I've got a shotgun."

Some of my guys were whispering to me that it wouldn't be a good idea to give them both barrels of a 12-gauge shotgun. People could get killed. The whole neighborhood would hear the shotgun blasts. Cops would be called. I'd be arrested and taken away.

I didn't care. I felt that I had to make a stand.

My show of force worked. The 18th Street guys got back in the Impala, each flipping me the bird. I chalked up that confrontation as a win and wasn't bothered again.

◆　◆　◆

It didn't take the administrative staff at Belmont High long to figure out who was the bad apple in the student body.

One scuffle too many got me transferred to Manual Arts, a downtown LA high school ruled by 18th Street. Several cafeteria fights later, I was shipped to Canoga Park High in the San Fernando Valley, which was a good hike from downtown LA. I had to take a long bus ride to school each day, which I hated. Being stuck in freeway traffic was a colossal waste of time.

A gang from South-Central LA called the Harpys, though few in number, ruled Canoga Park High. Gang members from downtown Los Angeles always considered the Valley gangs worthless. We even laughed at them, telling each other that we didn't even know they had gangs in San Fernando Valley. *You want real action? Then come to our neighborhoods.* Back where I lived, downtown LA was nicknamed "Home of the Body Bag." Most of the murders were committed by gang members between the ages of thirteen and sixteen—my age.

I wasn't at Canoga High long. I got kicked out after picking up a school chair—which was real heavy—and slamming a guy over the head for no other reason than he was part of the Harpys.

✦ ✦ ✦

The juvie authorities didn't know what to do with me, so they decided to try something new: ship me to Camp Miller, a youth detention camp in Malibu, one of the priciest zip codes in Los Angeles County. Camp Miller, located miles from the populated coastline in the foothills, was set in rustic surroundings.

Whenever I got into fights there—it was a matter of when, not if—I got sent next door to Camp Kilpatrick, a juvenile facility that contained solitary cells. Each time I was locked up in one of those cells, I was put into "the hole," as solitary confinement was called.

I was in the hole all the time. The usual "sentence" was two days and then it was back to Camp Miller, where I worked in the laundry room and on fire crew.

I didn't fight wild fires—you had to be eighteen years old to do that—but I worked on firebreaks during the summer months. Under a blazing sun, I'd hack at brush and weeds to create a strip of open space along a ridgeline or buck up fallen trees for removal. I actually liked the exercise and getting some fresh air.

While at Camp Miller, I got some bad news: Pedro, who jumped me into Rockwood, was shot to death in a gang ambush. The story was that a girl said she wanted to meet him and lured him to a nearby park, but it was all a setup. He had barely stepped out of his truck when a hail of bullets took him out.

Pedro had been a father figure. He meant everything to me, but now he was gone, just like Rabbit, who had coached me on my first stabbing. Before I arrived at Camp Miller, Rabbit was knifed in the stomach and did not survive. His death was a major shock to me at the time. I recall attending his funeral at a downtown mortuary, where he lay in an open casket. When I paid my respects, I peeked inside the casket. He didn't look like the same person. His face was a pasty color, and his features had changed. I remember looking at him and thinking, *Is that it? That's all?*

A feeling of ambivalence swept over me. During the funeral I saw people weeping: his mother, his sister, his girlfriend, and even some of our homeboys. As much as I tried to sympathize or console them, I couldn't raise the necessary emotions of empathy.

Despite the initial shock of Rabbit's murder—followed by Pedro's assassination—I reached a point where I wasn't bothered by the deaths of my homies. My attitude: *If you die, you die.* I didn't see the point of getting mushy or all sentimental; I had gotten used to death being a constant in my life.

There was another big reason why I didn't fuss about losing my brothers, and it was because I didn't think anybody in the whole world—except for my mom—cared whether I lived or got killed the next day.

If you die, you die.

✦ ✦ ✦

The part of gangbanging I liked the most was taking out rival gang members. Beyond the stealing and dealing drugs, the gang life was all about protecting your turf and settling scores. That necessitated violence, which was starting to feel like part of my DNA. In a few short years, I had become accustomed to brutality, barbarity, and brutishness.

Very early one Sunday morning, several Rockwood homies and

I were driving in one of our neighborhoods around one o'clock. We were hoping to spot any rival gang members slipping.

Slipping means they were out of their neighborhoods and roaming the streets—streets that were part of our territory.

"Looks like an MS-13, slipping on the right," one of my homies said from the back of a Toyota sedan. I was riding shotgun in the front passenger seat, as befitting my status. We had a driver and three guys in the back.

MS-13 guys were easy to spot: in those days, they wore long hair, black heavy-metal jackets, black T-shirts of their favorite bands, and tight black pants. On this evening, the gang member looked like he could answer a Hollywood casting call for an MS-13 gang member. (Today, MS-13 gang members look totally different: it's all about loose pants and head-to-toe tattoos.)

I had an idea. "Let's roll up and tell him we're with Easy Riders," I said. The Easy Riders were an offshoot of the Sureño street gang and affiliated with MS-13. If I told him we were Easy Riders, maybe he wouldn't run away.

And that would make it a lot easier for us to capture and waste him.

We rolled up real quiet as the MS 13 dude walked on the sidewalk, head down. When he turned a corner into a dark side street, I knew this was our chance. Careful not to spook him, we pulled up alongside him. I rolled down my window just as he realized that he had been followed. Startled by the presence of five homies stuffed in a Toyota two-door, he was about to hoof it—

"Hey, homie," I said soothingly. "We're with Easy Riders."

The MS-13 gang member stopped in his tracks. I hopped out of the car to greet him with my right hand extended. The guys in the back seat were on my heels.

He shook my hand, still wary.

And then we jumped him. I stepped aside as my guys whaled on him, sending him to the street pavement. Then they pounded him with their fists, followed by heavy kicks to the kidneys and stomping him in the head. It was a brutal beating, one that softened him up for what was to come.

I reached for a big screwdriver in my front pocket.

"Turn him around," I ordered.

The MS-13 gang member was curled up and practically comatose from the beating. My guys had kicked him pretty good on his head and face.

A couple of homies turned him onto his stomach.

What happened next is difficult to write, but I began stabbing the defenseless gang member in the back, in the neck, and high in the shoulder with a Phillips screwdriver. In my thirst for violence, I lost it and thrust the pointed end of the screwdriver through skin and sinew time after time.

Blood spattered everywhere and got all over my hands and clothes. I don't know how many times I pierced his skin, but it had to be more than a half dozen times.

We piled back into the Toyota and left him in the street.

It was getting late. My guys dropped me off at my parents' apartment. While saying goodbye, my driver appraised me.

"You better wash up," he said. "There's a lot of blood on your face."

I tiptoed up the stairs to our apartment. I was putting my key in the lock when suddenly the front door flew open. My mother was standing there in a bathrobe.

She placed her hands on her face in shock. "What happened to you?" she asked.

"There was a fight," I said.

"Look at all the blood on you!"

"Blood?" I was playing dumb.

"Yeah, blood. Let me show you."

I followed my mother to our only bathroom. Mom flipped on the switch, and I looked in the mirror. Blood was splattered on the side of my face from the temple to the jaw line, all over my shirt, and on my hands.

"What happened?" she asked again.

I ignored her and continued to look at the bloody face in the mirror—with a look I barely recognized.

"Relax, Mom. I'm going to be okay."

"You mean you didn't get stabbed?"

So that was why she was so upset. My mother thought I had been on the receiving end of a street knife.

"No, I didn't get stabbed. Can I take a shower now?"

My mother appeared relieved. "Sure," she said, closing the door and giving me privacy.

The first thing I did was wash my face and hands. I scrubbed my skin and watched the crimson-colored water drain down the sink.

Then I turned on the shower and started peeling off my clothes. I didn't want to wait until the water warmed up, like I did when I took a regular shower. Instead I hopped in the shower while the water was still warming up, feeling like I had to have a cold shower for some reason.

I held my shirt under the spray of cool water. The water at my feet was light red from all the blood that washed out of the shirt. When I wrung it out, the water became a deeper red.

After washing up, I stepped out of the bathroom with a towel wrapped around my waist.

"What's going on?" my mother asked.

"Nothing," I replied. "I got into a fight with somebody and busted him pretty good."

Mom gave me a look that I have never forgotten—a look that said, *I don't believe you. There's too much blood for you to have been only involved in a fight.*

"Mom, don't worry. It's all good. You can settle down."

My mother threw up her hands. It was too late to push further.

In those days before social media, it's hard to explain how it was possible for news to get around the neighborhood about the gruesome stabbing, but it seemed like everyone in the neighborhood heard what I had done. Well, maybe not everyone but certainly most of my male peers.

The following afternoon, I was walking through our neighborhood. Something was different: more than a few guys my age were chasing me down or coming out of the shadows to have a word with me. I felt like the godfather at a wedding reception.

These guys are really looking up to me.

I'm telling you, when life and death is in your hands, you feel really important.

And that's how I felt at the age of sixteen.

Invincible.

chapter six

GETTING MY LICKS IN

I don't know what made me so reckless on the street. I don't know why I valued life so little, including my own.

Maybe it was because when I made my bones as a gang member, I was all in. Maybe I had this drive to be different, to stand alone in a crowd. Maybe I was an out-of-control sixteen-year-old teen, pumped up with testosterone.

I believe two things drove me:

- I strived for recognition from my peers.
- I loved seeing fear in the eyes of other gang members, even my own.

But my thirst for blood came with a price, and the costly levy was that I had to do things the next guy wasn't willing to do. I'll leave it to your imagination what they were.

When you're part of a gang, the cycle of violence never ends. They take out one of yours; you take out one of theirs. Or you take out one of theirs, and they take out one of yours. Who started it had been long forgotten.

One time, one of our homeboys got jumped and roughed up pretty bad. My blood boiled when I heard that Spider received a savage beating from 18th Street gang members hanging out in the 3rd and Kenmore area. My homie took a battering, leaving him black and blue.

This was a big deal in my world. "They can't do that to Spider. We're going to show them who's boss!" I crowed.

◆　◆　◆

Four of us hopped into a lowrider for the drive to an 18th Street stronghold. Two were brothers; the other was Alejandro, thirteen years old and hoping to get jumped into Rockwood. He was excited to be cruising with us, and I could tell he looked up to me. In my young mind, I thought he should respect my position in the gang. Already I saw myself as a mentor to the young guys getting jumped in.

We were cruising through the 3rd and Kenmore neighborhood when I noticed an 18th Street gang member hanging out on the door-step of a semi-abandoned building, sipping on a "forty" wrapped in a brown paper bag. Everything in the way he was dressed said he was from 18th Street. The fact that he was alone caught my eye, much like how a mountain lion on the prowl spots an unprotected fawn in the forest.

I leaned out of the passenger's seat and shouted, "Eighteen rules!"

In other words, I was claiming I was an 18th Street member, repeating a tactic that I had used dozens of times. I didn't want him to run. He was my prey.

He stopped a long draw from the oversized bottle of beer, wiping his mouth with the back of his hand. He didn't move when I stepped out of the car, but his eyes locked on my right hand, where I gripped a long screwdriver. Once he spotted my weapon, he dropped the forty and immediately began sprinting down the street. The chase was on.

"Stay here!" I yelled to Blackie. What was going to happen was gang business, and he hadn't been jumped in yet. The other two homies—the brothers—were ready for some action.

We sprinted after the 18th Street gang member with me leading the way. He ran past several houses until he came upon a small apartment complex, two stories tall. He looked like he knew where he was going because he ran straight to one of the units. The front door was open, protected by a screen door.

I was closing in fast. Before he could slam the front door in my face and lock it, I barged into the small living room. A couple of men and an older woman leaped up from a pair of tattered couches, wearing shocked expressions on their faces. They quickly retreated to the kitchen like scared kittens. I wasn't concerned with them. There was only one thing on my mind—revenge.

My mark—the 18th Street gang member—sensed that he was in the fight for his life. With hands up in supplication, he begged, "No, man . . . don't do this, man." He continued to back up until he clumsily tripped over a coffee table, falling on his stomach.

Down on the ground, scared out of his skin, and in a weakened state, my prey was ready to be slaughtered. I jumped on top of the dude and started stabbing him. I slashed him in the head and punctured him in the neck and back. I don't remember how many times I stabbed him, but it was probably ten or fifteen times. I was an absolute animal. I don't know why I wanted to kill him, but I wanted him gone. I kept raising my right arm and savagely delivered stabbing after stabbing.

"My son, my son, no, no, my son!" an older woman screamed. Neither she nor the two men attempted to stop me, however; perhaps they sensed they would be next if they interfered.

When I was done doing what I had to do, I got up and screamed,

"@#$% 18!" Then I looked over to one of the brothers. He was being helpful by holding open the screen door.

"Time to go," I announced.

Once again, we sprinted back to the car and hopped in, where Alejandro was waiting. One of the brothers got behind the wheel and slammed his foot on the gas pedal. The Chevy engine roared to life. Tires screeched, and we got out of there, burnt rubber filling our nostrils.

I was sitting shotgun, holding a blood-drenched screwdriver in my hands, which were a bloody mess.

I turned around to Alejandro, who was sitting in the back seat, eyes as big as saucers.

"You want in?" I asked. "This is how you get in."

And then I raised the bloody screwdriver to my mouth and licked it. Not once but twice.

I'll never forget the look on Alejandro's face—full of terror.

I chuckled to release the tension. "Don't worry about the other guy," I said. "He's resting comfortably."

Actually, I heard the guy from 18th survived the brutal attack. But he would never walk again—he was paralyzed.

✦ ✦ ✦

It sounds unbelievable to write this, but I was proud I did that to him. In the brutal world of LA street gangs, there was a war being fought in the neighborhoods. Just as there was in any war, there would be casualties. That was the risk you took when you jumped in. I couldn't let down my Rockwood homies, not after I was in this deep. If anything, my disregard for life had become more intense, more brazen, and more defiant.

What about the screams of a desperate mother begging for her son's life? They didn't register with me. I totally tuned her out. Her son too. Nothing affected me.

My conscience was gone.

My soul had turned black.

✦   ✦   ✦

I had many run-ins with other gangs but mostly with 18th Street. We just never seemed to get along. But in a war with no end, that didn't matter.

I didn't need to pump myself up with drugs or get drunk to go on a rampage; I was sober, solemn, and serious during each assault. Most of the time, my attacks were not premeditated. I was just responding to provocations that came my way.

Like the time a bunch of 18th Street gang members arrived by van in a Rockwood neighborhood. Well, maybe it wasn't officially our territory, but did it matter? They were in our space, and they brought along some *chicas* with them. It was a big group.

We ran into them as they were walking around a run-down commercial district. They were laughing and having fun, flashing hand signs to "claim" the neighborhood for 18th Street. They used the fingers of the right hand to form a capital "E" for 18th Street.

I happened to be walking to a friend's apartment with some of my homies when we ran into this renegade bunch with girls hanging all over them.

The leader ticked me off. I didn't like the way he looked or carried himself. Such an attitude.

"We're 18th Street, man," he spouted off. "Nuthin' you can do about it."

Normally, I give guys a pass if they mouth off once, maybe twice. But this gang leader kept going on and on about how 18th was the greatest and no one could touch them. I'm not sure when my fuse got lit, but when it happened, I roared off the launch pad on a mission of mayhem.

Before I rushed him, I reached for a screwdriver in the back of my baggy Levi's 501s. Or maybe it was an ice pick. No, I'm pretty sure it was a screwdriver.

I charged. His dukes went up—but not in time. I swung with my right hand and jammed the screwdriver into his left eye.

Blood squirted out, and he screeched. Normally my victims screamed, but this was not a normal scream. This was a freak-out: a screech to the high heavens. What was even grosser was that the screwdriver remained in the eye socket.

"He stabbed me in the eye! He stabbed me in the eye!" This guy was in such pain.

After he fell to the sidewalk, I don't remember what happened next. Chaos, I guess.

Bodies came out of nowhere, including several armed security guards. I don't know why they were in the vicinity, but they were. Two of them slammed me to the ground, and the next thing I knew, I was handcuffed and led into a building, where I was taken to some sort of barren security room with monitors.

"Shut up! Don't say anything!" said one of the security guards, taking control of the situation.

Security guards brought in more handcuffed gang members— from 18th Street *and* Rockwood. One wasn't handcuffed—the 18th Street rival that I wounded with a thrust to his left eye. The screwdriver had been removed. He held his left hand over his eye, but blood seeped between his fingers. His head was lowered, and he appeared to be fighting to remain standing.

Just as quickly as the victim was led to this security room, he was taken away.

I wondered what was going to happen next. Actually, I knew the jig was up: I would be handed over to the LAPD and charged with attempted murder. I was doing time for this. But I didn't care.

I sat in this chair for another twenty minutes, pondering my fate. Then out of nowhere, an armed security guard—a new one—came into the dungeon-like room.

"Stand up," he said.

I obeyed his command.

"Turn around."

I complied.

I heard the jangle of keys, and then he unlocked the handcuffs.

"What's going on?" I asked, shaking my wrists to boost circulation. My hands were pretty numb.

"Get out of here," he barked.

Another security guard opened up a door that led to the rear parking lot.

"Go," he directed. "Before the cops get here."

I don't know why he let me go. Maybe they had run-ins with the 18th Street gang members and thought they deserved some comeuppance. That's the only reason that made sense to me. They had me dead to rights: handcuffed and ready to be handed over to the LAPD. But they let me go.

I ran into a dark parking lot, alone. This was not good. I couldn't be walking around this neighborhood. I'm sure there was an APB—all-points bulletin—on me by both the LAPD and 18th Street. The former would lock me up; the latter would kill me.

And then I saw a van in the back of the parking lot—one of ours. Talk about a welcome sight! I ran over to the vehicle, giddy with delight. A van door slid open, and I jumped in.

Relief prompted a release of laughter. "That's how you do it," I chortled. "That's how you do it."

The way I did it was by destroying my enemies before they destroyed me.

✦ ✦ ✦

As you've been reading along, you probably have the impression that gang members spend all their time claiming territory and maiming and killing their rivals. While that's an important part of gang life, we also spent a lot of time stealing through breaking and entering into people's homes and apartments. That's how we made some money to buy gas and food or trick up our rides with lowrider suspensions or new upholstery.

They weren't called home invasions back then, but we were the guys invading their space. Whenever we broke into someone's place, I *wanted* those living there to be home. I always thought it was cowardly to break into an empty house and ransack someone's jewelry box or rifle through drawers looking for cash with no one around. I preferred to tie up the frightened renters or homeowners with duct tape, point a gun at them, and ask where their valuables were.

You would be surprised how cooperative people were in those stressful situations. It was also a much more efficient way to rob them. Plus I liked the feeling of taking over a place, duct-taping people scared out of their wits, and then walking away with anything of value.

By the time I was sixteen, I was doing a lot of robberies. I mean every day, every night, and sometimes as many as three or four robberies in a day. As we picked through our territory, I had the brilliant idea of going to Koreatown and robbing those people. A lot of Asians owned businesses and kept money at home because they didn't trust the banks—plus it was a cash economy, just like in our hood.

One night I filled a car with some of my guys for a little road trip to Koreatown. We were scoping out a walk-up apartment block when I saw an older Hispanic lady, probably in her forties or fifties, sitting in an electric wheelchair on a street corner. As we drove by, she signaled for us to pull over.

"Do it," I said to my driver. "Let's see what she's got." I wondered why a Hispanic lady was in this part of town, sitting in a wheelchair under a streetlamp. Our car pulled up alongside her.

"How much do you want?" she asked, an obvious indication that she was dealing drugs, even though she was crippled and unable to walk.

"We want a large party," I said. Why I said that, I don't know. I guess I wanted to see how things played out.

"You got money?"

"Yeah, we got money," I replied.

I dug into my front pocket and extracted a roll of cash. "I'm not here for a dime or anything like that," I said, meaning ten dollars' worth of weed. "I want a lot of stuff."

"Give me a second," she said.

I watched her wheel herself into an apartment building. The minutes passed by slowly. Then, about ten minutes later, she returned.

"They want to see you," she said.

"Who wants to see me?"

"A guy. He's with 18th Street."

Now things were getting interesting. Not only were we going to cross paths with a rival gang member, but this could be a chance to rob him and take his drugs, which had to be worth thousands of dollars on the street.

We held the upper hand, I believed, because we were strapped, meaning we had guns. I had a sawed-off shotgun in my lap, and my guys carried handguns. I usually didn't carry a gun with me, preferring to render violence with a tool in my hand—usually a Phillips screwdriver. Nonetheless, I stuffed the sawed-off shotgun into my waistband and followed the older woman as she wheeled herself into a ground-floor apartment.

The first thing I saw were pillowcases on the living room floor, with Ziploc bags filled with white powder spilling out of them. The drugs had to be crack cocaine. A guy sitting on a couch was stuffing bags of crack into a pillowcase. Another guy was standing next to a kitchen counter, where I saw several stacks of bundled-up cash and a weight scale. There was also a heavy-looking handgun. So there were more guys and more weapons than I expected.

I made my move. I took the loaded shotgun out of my pants and rushed the guy on the couch. With my shotgun pointed at his face, I yelled, "Who else is here?"

The other dude at the kitchen counter started to reach for his gun—

"If you pick that up, I'm blowing your homeboy's head off," I announced. "Then I'm coming after you."

He backed away from the kitchen counter, but I wasn't going to take any chances.

"On your knees!" I demanded.

He immediately acquiesced. With arms on top of his head, he knelt down in a supplicant position. Then I stepped up to him and placed the end of the sawed-off shotgun in his mouth to let him know that I really meant business.

When I removed the weapon from his mouth, he started to whimper. "Please don't kill me! Please don't kill me! I'll do anything you want!"

I wasn't going to kill him or his partner. Shooting people wasn't my thing. I just wanted to put fear into these guys, and I succeeded. The woman in the wheelchair? She was crippled and remained outside the apartment, watched by one of my guys.

We started ransacking the place. We found bundles of money. We found more dope. And then we escaped with our haul, laughing the entire way.

This robbery was almost too easy.

I really believed no one could touch me.

chapter seven

IN HOT PURSUIT

Not long after I ripped off several drug dealers in Koreatown, gang warfare broke out between Rockwood and 18th Street—and there was a body count to prove it.

The cycle of violence never broke, which kept everyone on a razor's edge. There was no way I could trust anyone connected with 18th Street, and I know the feeling was mutual. Since I had many run-ins with 18th Street gangbangers, I kept my head on a swivel.

One early evening, while it was still light, I pulled into the parking lot of Dino's, a hole-in-the-wall fried chicken and burger joint on Pico Boulevard. I was hungry and wanted something to eat.

The nothing-fancy restaurant contained eight Formica tables with uncomfortable vinyl chairs, but Dino's had a cult-like following because of their tasty food. I was there for their humongous burgers and DUI fries—chili cheese fries with carne asada, pastrami, cheese, and Dino's sauce. Lots of good grease, and it was cheap.

The restaurant was quiet; I was the only customer before the dinner crowd arrived. I was biting into my charbroiled burger and sampling the chili cheese fries when I looked up and noticed a half dozen gangbangers rushing the entrance door. I immediately recognized them as being from 18th Street.

My heart rate immediately shot up. This wasn't a social call. I knew 18th Street had a big interest in getting rid of me. There was unfinished business between us.

The lead guy with 18th Street brandished a nasty-looking crowbar in his right hand, and three other guys flexed baseball bats on their shoulders, ready to swing away.

I reacted automatically. When the 18th Street crew rushed me, I pushed my table into their path and grabbed a chair to protect myself. I immediately regretted not carrying a gun. I didn't have a knife on me—or even a screwdriver.

It suddenly hit me that I was in the midst of a life-or-death situation: the 18th Street gangbangers were bent on cracking open my head and watching me bleed to death while they walked away, laughing like hyenas. With adrenaline coursing through my veins, I fended off a swing of the crowbar and thrust a chair at another attacker, who was swinging for the fences. I blocked his heavy bat and tied him up momentarily, which gave me a second to escape.

I knew my only chance was to get to the streets. I zigzagged like an open-field running back and sprinted for the restaurant entrance. Once past the front door, I raced for my car parked in front of the restaurant. I was driving a beat-up Toyota Corolla, an unremarkable four-door sedan that looked like a zillion other imports on the streets of LA.

The guy with the crowbar remained in hot pursuit, even though I was fast as lightning, thanks to being five feet, seven inches tall and weighing only 105 pounds. Throughout the hood I was known for being quick on my feet—especially when a half-crazed guy wielding a deadly weapon was chasing me.

The attacker was just steps behind me so I didn't have time to open the driver's door and jump in. Being short and skinny made it easy to leap through the open window on the driver's side, which I did. Then, on my stomach, I reached under the passenger's seat.

My right hand quickly found what I was looking for: an H&R single-shot, break-action shotgun. This was an old-school 12-gauge shotgun that broke into two pieces—a short twenty-four-inch barrel and a pistol-grip stock that contained the firing and trigger mechanism. The shotgun, which was loaded, fired one shell at a time.

I gripped the shotgun and turned on my back. The 18th Street gangbanger leaned through the driver's window, screaming, "You @#$% @#$$!" In a rage, he thrust the crowbar into my face—

And that's when I pulled the trigger.

There was an explosion, and I saw his body jerk and land in a heap next to the driver's door. The ear-splitting sound of the shotgun reverberated throughout the neighborhood. I heard screams and shouts of panic as I pulled myself out of the car and took measure of the situation. The 18th Street gang member was sprawled on the pavement, a gigantic red gash on his upper chest and neck. He was bleeding profusely and lying still.

I calmly reached into my right pocket and found what I was looking for—another 12-gauge shell. I broke open the shotgun and smoothly removed the empty shell and inserted the new one. I didn't hesitate: I shot him again. If he wasn't dead before, he was now. I had no problem rationalizing what I had done: I wasn't looking for it, didn't want it, but the circumstances came to me. I did what had to be done.

Keep in mind that this all happened in broad daylight. I preferred to even the score under the cover of darkness, but this was different. Now there were too many witnesses, but I couldn't do anything about them.

That's why I had to lay low. For the next week or two, I couch-surfed at homes of fellow gang members. Then one of my homies said the duplex he was living in had an abandoned unit, so I stayed there. The creature comforts weren't much—just a moldy old mattress and a chair or two—but his mother fed me. I was taken care of.

I knew the cops were on the lookout for me. One of the LA newspapers, the *Los Angeles Herald-Examiner*, even ran a police sketch that kind of resembled what I looked like. I needed to get out of town, so we came up with a plan: one of my homies would drive me to Vegas, where I would sit tight until the heat died down.

✦   ✦   ✦

Just before I was supposed to leave for Las Vegas, I got a call from Blanco—a white-looking Mexican from a gang we got along with.

Blanco was a cool guy and someone I had worked with in the past. He had heard on the streets that I was leaving for Vegas to lay low, so he took it upon himself to organize a going-away party for me.

"You'd really do that for me?" I said when I received the news.

"Sure, homie. You don't think your bros would forget you, do you?"

"I guess not." In a weird sort of way, I was touched, which was unusual for me. I normally stuffed down any feelings I had for others—except for those in my gang.

"Is tomorrow night going to be okay?" he asked.

I didn't see any problem with that. Laying low also meant my social calendar was wide open.

And then I remembered something.

"Can you meet me later today?" I asked.

"How come?"

"I want to ask you something, but I have to do it in person."

"Listen, Casey, if you're—"

"No, I'm not thinking along those lines at all. It's just a little favor."

Blanco hesitated, probably because he knew me too well, but I convinced him to take the meeting. We agreed to meet at an apartment complex on Normandie Street at four o'clock.

Normandie Street, in Westlake between East Hollywood and Koreatown, was a plumb line for a Latino neighborhood populated by aging bungalows and low-slung apartment buildings. We met under a carport at the apartment complex to get out of the sun as well as stay away from any prying eyes.

I thanked him for organizing a gathering on my behalf, and then I came to the real reason I wanted to see him.

"Can you hold these until tonight?" I asked.

Before Blanco could say anything, I reached into my waist and extracted two handguns—a .357 snub-nose pistol and a .38 revolver. They weren't automatics, but they were powerful pistols that could stop a rhinoceros in its tracks.

Blanco stared at the bulky handguns, which weren't to be trifled with.

"Just make sure you don't get caught with them, because they're hot," I said.

Blanco's easy demeanor turned serious. A "hot gun" meant that I could have used it recently in the commission of a serious crime. Which was true.

Blanco palmed the weapons and then put them away in his pants pockets. "Whatever you say, man," he replied.

I fished into my pockets and found a handful of bullets. "Here, you better keep these too."

We exchanged a handshake and were off. Accompanied by two Rockwood homies, I turned and walked northbound on Normandie, which had a slight rise. We all heard the noise at the same time—the whirring of helicopter blades. I looked to the skies and saw a white LAPD police helicopter with blue trim lazily hanging in the air. The chopper wasn't directly over us. In fact, the helicopter was a ways off but hovered in the same place.

"Hey, they're probably looking for you," one of my buddies joked, and we shared a laugh.

"Nah, he wants *you*," I teased back.

I didn't think the LAPD chopper was *specifically* looking for me. A month had passed since the violent encounter at Dino's—practically an eternity on the mean streets of LA. The cops were on to other homicides. It seemed like every day another gang member was pushing up daisies. What happened between the gangbanger from 18th Street and me was between us and would stay that way.

We made a right on Oakwood and headed east toward the San Gabriel Mountains ringing downtown LA. I saw a place between apartment buildings to sit down and hang out, talk about things. We plunked ourselves down on some steps in front of a wooden fence when suddenly the entire Rampart Division of the Los Angeles Police Department converged on the neighborhood. At least, that's what it seemed like to me. Five cop cars rushed toward us and came to a halt. A lady cop jumped out of the passenger seat of one of the cruisers and stood behind the passenger door. Then the cruiser advanced very slowly toward us.

The lady cop raised a shotgun and made eye contact with me. "If you move one inch, I'm going to blow your @#$% head off," she yelled.

Her shotgun wasn't the only firearm aimed in my direction. I'd say a dozen cops had taken position next to their squad cars and had trained pistols on my homies and me.

For a fleeting second, I thought I could jump the fence behind me and give them an exciting chase, but knowing that Rampart was on the scene, such a move would have been fatal. I raised my hands in surrender.

"On the @#$% ground!" yelled one cop.

I knew the drill. With hands raised high, I kneeled, laid on my stomach, and placed my hands behind my back. I almost immediately felt the cold steel of the handcuffs clamp shut and then probing hands and fingers reach into my pockets, waistband, pants inseam, and lower legs. Then a rope-like device came around my wrists and ankles. I was hog-tied.

Next thing I knew I was hoisted into the air. A burly LAPD cop picked me up with the ropes and dumped me into the back of the lady cop's cruiser. I would later learn she was the lead detective on my case.

I was tossed into the back seat like a sack of dirty laundry and landed on the vinyl seating with a thud. I struggled to become upright, but I couldn't move.

I was driven to the Rampart Police Station on West 6th and interviewed for several hours. I didn't tell the cops anything, and I certainly didn't betray my gang, but the evidence that I killed another gangbanger at Dino's restaurant portended an open-and-shut case.

I was given a public defender who went through the motions. Meanwhile, I stayed behind bars because I was deemed a risk to the community, which I was. Within a few months, I had my day in court.

When it was all over, I got tagged with a second-degree murder rap and was sentenced by the Los Angeles Superior Court to a twelve-year, eight-month term for second-degree murder and *fifty-two* counts of armed robbery. I actually breathed a sigh of relief that those were the only charges the cops could pin on me.

✦　✦　✦

Since I was sixteen and still considered a minor, I was notified that I would serve the first two years in juvenile detention facilities run by the California Youth Authority. When I turned eighteen, I would become eligible to be transferred to the "big house"—an adult prison. Conceivably, I would have ten years left on my prison term when that happened.

At an age when most kids are getting their first driver's license, I was shipped off to Ventura School, a juvenile maximum-security correctional facility run by the CYA in Camarillo, midway between Los Angeles and Santa Barbara.

◆ ◆ ◆

Adapting to prison life wasn't too bad. The chow was okay, and I could go to school. Since I already had my high school diploma, having earned one at continuation school prior to my arrest (I was kicked out of Belmont High School because of my gang involvement), I took college classes and earned forty-two units at Ventura School by the time I turned eighteen.

Turning eighteen isn't a time for celebration when you're stuck in a prison cell. I couldn't help but think about my teen peers, who look forward to their eighteenth birthdays because that's when the world says you're an adult. You can vote, buy a house, purchase a gun, or marry your childhood sweetheart. In a handful of states, you can legally drink or buy medical marijuana. You're making plans for college or deciding what you're going to do in life.

Turning eighteen meant something entirely different to me. Hitting that magic age signified that the California penal system could now treat me like an adult, which meant locking me up with adult offenders. In recognition of that new reality, I was transferred from Ventura School to YTS—Youth Training School—in Chino, east of LA. It's a CYA facility for those who've turned eighteen and are waiting to be processed into adult prison. TS wasn't much of a school, though. They didn't teach me anything. I sat in a cell all day.

I was in TS for a short stay, under six months. Then I was transferred to Men's Central Jail in downtown LA, where I would stay until I was handed over to the state prison system. At Men's Central, the LA County sheriff's deputies kept me in a gang module for obvious reasons. I still remember where I was locked down: Denver Row, Module 3400. (Denver stands for D—as in A for Alpha and B for Bravo, and so on.)

This was my first time housed in an adult prison population, and the differences were stark. In CYA or juvenile hall, you looked for fellow gang members and stuck together. You had to because the gangs were still fighting each other in the juvenile jails.

But once you got to the adult level, as I learned at Men's Central, divisions between gangs disappeared, and all the Latino gangbangers united and became one. It didn't matter if I had killed one of your brothers or someone in your family or that you were part of a rival Latino gang—everything changed when we met up in prison. You were my teammate and I was yours, and that was it.

The same mentality permeated the white and black prisoner population: *You stick with your kind.* You did that to protect yourself. Maybe things evolved that way because you naturally trusted people who looked like you and came from the same background—or spoke the same language. Whatever the reason, a "we're in this together" mind-set was tangible within prison walls. Banding in unison also made sense when you had a long sentence ahead of you   ten, twenty, or thirty years. You needed allies if you were going to survive and ever see the outside again.

Another thing I learned in the adult prison system is that you never know how long you're going to stay inside a certain lock-up. One morning, they'll call out your name and "roll you up," as prisoners call it, and ship you to another correctional facility. That's what happened to me after two months inside the gang module at Men's Central Jail. Suddenly one day I was rolled up and bused to the Peter J. Pitchess Detention Center, an all-male Los Angeles County correctional facility in Castaic, north of LA's San Fernando Valley near Magic Mountain. The twenty-six-hundred-acre concrete-and-razor-wire prison was filled to the brim with nearly nine thousand men.

Like most penal institutions, inmates had a different name for the Pitchess Detention Center. We called it Wayside because it was nicknamed the Wayside Drunk Farm back in the 1940s when most inmates found themselves there for alcohol-related offenses. I was put into the 2400 East Max wing of Wayside with 120 guys, and I'd say that around 85 percent were murderers. The rest were violent criminals.

At Wayside, just like with Men's Central, we segregated ourselves: blacks aligning with blacks, whites aligning with whites, and browns—the Latinos—aligning with browns.

I quickly met a bunch of Latino gang members in my wing, including dudes from two long-established gangs: 18th Street and Florencia 13—a.k.a. F13 or Florence 13—from South-Central LA.

I've already described how in Los Angeles 18th Street was a transnational gang with tens of thousands of members. As for F13, their leadership came from the rolls of the Mexican Mafia. They kept a tight grip on their turf by shooting rival Latino and black gang members plus black civilians who happened to be in the wrong place at the wrong time.

Back in LA, we'd be at each other's throats, but inside state prison, rival gang members welcomed me, and they made my transition into Wayside as comfortable as possible.

◆　◆　◆

I learned an important lesson on my fourth day at Wayside, and it started when the Crips—an African American gang who traditionally wore blue clothing in South-Central LA—approached us Latinos with a question. I was included in the discussion, which shows you how quickly I established rank among my peers.

The Crips said they wanted to "charge tax" on some of the white guys in our unit. "Charge tax" meant that they wanted to do whatever they wanted to these white guys, but they wanted to make sure that none of us Latinos "owned" any of them. In other words, the Crips didn't want to mess with us because if any of the white guys were owned by us, they weren't allowed to touch them. The Crips were cautious about this because such a move could set off a riot, which would mean trouble for them.

Like I said, the Crips approached us, told us what they were up to, and we gave them the go-ahead. Within the hour, they were going from bunk to bunk, doing heavy damage to the white folks inside Wayside. That's how things rolled in prison.

I was lying in my bunk, reading a book, and trying not to pay attention to the mayhem around me. I had gotten good at compartmentalizing myself during two, three years of prison life. Behind my bunk was a low-slung wall. From beyond the barrier, I heard a man desperately screaming, "No! No! Don't!"

I turned my head slightly to see what the commotion was about. I noticed seven or eight black guys standing in a semicircle. A white guy must have been on the floor, lying face down. They took turns raping him, each encounter eliciting another round of blood-curdling screams. It was sickening.

I tried to focus on my book, but in my mind, I was thinking, *This is real. This is really happening.* I was amazed how ruthless these people could be.

◆　◆　◆

I certainly didn't want to end up like that poor guy behind the barrier. I stayed on my toes, and then I caught a break. Several guys approached me and asked me to become a "shot caller"—the person calling the shots—in 2400 East Max.

Shot callers have an elevated rank in the gang world. Not only are they the ones commanding respect, but they don't have to carry out what will and will not happen. They are power brokers inside prison walls and determine who gets hurt or killed and who doesn't.

Shot callers have street cred, which is why I was approached. People already knew me from the streets, so when the previous shot caller was transferred to a different state prison, a leadership vacuum was created. I was asked to fill it.

One of the shot callers' responsibilities was to control the shanks within the prison population—the crude homemade knives used for stabbing another prisoner.

I became the one who slept with the shanks—all thirteen of them under my mattress. You may be wondering: *If I'm part of your gang, why would I give you my shank? Why give up that power?*

Here's my answer: when you're elected shot caller—after a vote is taken of the inmates you're aligned with—then you're to be respected. It would be suicidal not to give me your shank because if you don't, then you're done. I'll have you killed.

When a riot went off, I made sure the right people got shanks. There were many violent upheavals at Wayside, and inmates were getting stabbed and killed all the time. All it took was a wrong look at the wrong person, and you were done for. One careless act—even a reckless word—and your life was forfeited, usually in the dorm. Life was very cheap.

I was at Wayside for several months. Not only did I have a dozen shanks in my possession, but I also had access to Folgers coffee, Snickers bars, Camel cigarettes, cocaine, and even heroin. How was that possible for a prisoner in a California state prison?

Answer: because of the cooperation of attorneys and prison guards.

Let's talk about the attorneys first. Whenever a lawyer visits a prisoner, the law stipulates that he or she cannot be searched . . . or searched very closely. The criminal defense attorney must pass through a metal detector to make sure that a gun is not on his person, but he is not patted down, nor is his briefcase emptied out on a table. There are perfunctory searches, but that's about it.

Because of this loophole, all sorts of stuff and contraband breach the prison walls.

Are that many defense attorneys crooked? No, not at all, but they are subject to . . . pressure. Pressure from gang leaders on the outside. Pressure to cooperate.

The same thing can be said for prison guards. No guard *willingly* smuggles in cigarettes or drugs like heroin to prisoners—but some do it for the right price. For those who can't be bought, some can be coerced into cooperating through threats and intimidation.

Not by prisoners, of course, but what happens is a gang member on the outside will visit a guard's home and knock on his or her door one evening to shoot the breeze . . . and leave behind a subtle threat that collaboration would be a healthy idea for both sides. Guards who appear weak are targeted for this steel-hand-in-a-velvet-glove approach. Others are dealt with in more direct terms: *We know who you are, we obviously know where you and your family live, and you're going to work for us.*

And that's how a lot of stuff got smuggled into 2400 East Max.

One of my favorite ways to conceal a shank was to place it inside a toilet rim. That may sound incredibly gross sticking your hands all the way inside a toilet, but you do what you have to do.

Another creative method used to move things around prison was a practice called "keistering," also known as "putting it in the safe" or "packing the rabbit." Keistering meant hiding things in the alley-oop—the anus. I knew guys keistering prison-made shanks as long as a six-inch ruler inside their rectums. Sure, they were sharp and the practice was insanely dangerous, but the attitude in prison is that you're going to do it, so that's it.

Keistering was also the way drugs were smuggled into prison by attorneys or "trustees" who concealed—in their briefcases—packages of cocaine or heroin that were wrapped in Reynolds aluminum foil and slathered with generous amounts of lubricant. Once handed to their clients, the prisoners then inserted the cache into their rectums and returned to their cells. I knew guys with five-thousand-dollars' worth of heroin in their possession. When I say five-thousand-dollars' worth, that's in prison currency. The heroin wouldn't be worth as much on the outside, but in prison, that was big money.

Thank goodness, I was in a position of strength where I didn't have to keister drugs or shanks.

◆　◆　◆

After my stay in Wayside, I was placed on a prison bus and driven to North Kern State Prison in Delano, twenty-five miles north of sunbaked Bakersfield in Central California, where I was evaluated for 120 days. This four-month period at North Kern State Prison gave the state penal system time to research my gang involvement or if I had any entanglements with organized crime. I also underwent a psychological evaluation and met with gang coordinators—those are the correctional officers who specialize in gangs outside and inside prisons. They had probably figured out that I was a shot caller at Wayside. They also reviewed my file for any offenses I had committed while in their custody or at CYA. All this information determined what level of security I would need inside a state prison.

Everything was based on a point system, 1 to 100. When everything was added up, I scored a 97. I wasn't surprised my number was that high. Actually, I was kind of proud.

I was a shot caller, remember?

chapter eight

EARLY RIDE

had been at North Kern State Prison for around six months when an unexpected wake-up call came at 4:00 a.m.

That's the thing about prison. Correction officers are always waking you up real early, long before daybreak. Maybe that's part of the punishment—rattling your cell bars with their black batons while you're dreaming about life on the outside. It sure felt that way to me.

I think the guards received some sort of perverse pleasure hearing prisoners moan from the lack of sleep or watching us struggle to open our eyes in the predawn darkness. Or maybe the guards discovered over the years that early wake-up calls made inmates more docile—and reminded us that we don't have control over any aspect of our lives.

Normally, I was rousted out of bed at 5:30 a.m. for roll call, but one fall morning a pair of noisy guards came just before daybreak. I soon learned the reason for their visit: I would be "catching a chain"—prison lingo for making a transfer—from North Kern State Prison to one of California's maximum-security state prisons. Which one? I didn't know. Prisoners were always the last to be told anything. For security reasons, I figured.

One of the guards handed me a red jumpsuit for the bus ride to a new state prison. Most of the time, inmates wear orange or navy blue jumpsuits, but I was singled out to wear red because of my gang background. I would find out later that day why scarlet was the new black—at least in the prison world.

Two guards cuffed me up and escorted me into a massive holding room that stank of sweat and urine. Probably two dozen prisoners were catching a chain that day. We lined up in two rows and stood in lackadaisical attention. I held a brown folder that I had purchased at the canteen—the prison store—and filled it with my court papers. I also stuffed a toothbrush, toothpaste, a travel-size shampoo, and a couple of snacks in the folder. That's all I was taking. I gave away everything else that was mine. I didn't see how I was going to need any of those things where I was going.

My nose detected a rank smell. Off to one side, a half dozen commodes were attached to a masonry wall. There were no partitions between the stainless-steel toilets, which were open for all to see. I noticed a couple of prisoners squatting and squirming to have a bowel movement; obviously their morning constitutional had arrived early. Another prisoner, with his back to me, sent a spray of urine into the silver commode.

"Anyone else for head call?" barked one of the guards.

Even though I had relieved myself before leaving my cell, I thought it would be a good idea to go again. Prison buses didn't have toilets on board, and I knew that the guards didn't make unscheduled stops so that cons could visit a gas station restroom. Good thing I did because for the next six hours, I wouldn't be allowed to go to the bathroom.

When I stepped back into line, the guards began prepping us for the long bus ride.

"Full restraints," a correctional officer bellowed, holding a blue milk crate filled with chains.

When it was my turn, a guard wrapped a set of chains—known as Martin chains or belly chains—around my waist, which were then locked to handcuffs around my wrists. Next, my ankles were shackled with leg irons that connected to my waist chain via another linked chain. Security boxes covered the restraints' keyholes. Prisoners called the entire get-up a "four-piece suit."

One of the guards overseeing the process approached me with a beige folder in his hands. He opened the manila portfolio, then gave me an up-and-down look.

"Darwin Diaz?" he asked.

I looked up. Only prison guards and schoolteachers called me by my legal name—Darwin Diaz. On the streets and behind bars, everyone referred to me by my nickname—Casey.

"What are you in here for?" he asked.

I knew his paperwork didn't reveal my crime or describe what I had been sentenced for. That information was mine, which meant I didn't have to answer him.

I shrugged and didn't offer a reply, but not in a defiant way. We both knew I didn't have to respond, so I let his question float in the air.

The guard moved on. "How old are you?" he asked.

Now, that was information he *did* have in his file. I figured he was curious why I looked so young. I was small in stature and didn't have any facial hair. Like most teens, I wanted to be *older* than I appeared to be.

"I'm eighteen, but I turn nineteen in a couple of weeks."

The guard wasn't impressed and barely disguised a look of contempt—as in *What a waste.* "You know where you're goin'?"

"I don't give a @#$%," I replied. Again, my matter-of-fact tone was respectful. You have to be deferential when dealing with the turtles, which is what we called guards since they dressed in olive green.

"Since you have ninety-seven points, you're going to Sac," he declared with a bit of relish.

So that's where I was headed. I gritted my teeth.

I had heard about "Sac"—shorthand for California State Prison, Sacramento, located in Folsom, approximately twenty miles northeast of the state capital in Sacramento. As one of thirty-three prisons operated by the California Department of Corrections and Rehabilitation, nobody referred to this notorious maximum security prison as "California State Prison, Sacramento." Instead, everyone—meaning the inmate population, the guards, and the prisoners' families—called this sprawling correctional facility "New Folsom" because the prison butted up next to Folsom State Prison, built in 1880 and made famous in the late 1960s by singer Johnny Cash, whose concert for the Folsom inmates was immortalized in the film *Walk the Line*.

New Folsom was brand-new, having opened a year earlier. The prison had three separate but similar self-contained sections that formed a 180-degree half circle—known in prison circles as a "180 design"—that gave guards overlooking the exercise yards and officers in the control booths a better chance to keep their eyes on prisoners. Right from the get-go, New Folsom was state-of-the-art and equipped to take the worst of the worst.

The news that I was headed to New Folsom weighed on my mind as I waited to be loaded onto the prison transport vehicle—a converted Greyhound bus known as the "Gray Goose." Painted an institutional green and having seen better days, the Gray Goose was what the state used to move prisoners around.

I had a surprise waiting for me as I boarded the Gray Goose in the company of a prison guard. Instead of sitting in one of the regular seats—which were slabs of metal—I was segregated from the other prisoners and placed inside a one-person cage on the right side of the bus as you walk down the aisle. The three individual cages on the prison bus reminded me of chicken coops. The reason I would have to ride in a cage was because I was deemed too dangerous to sit next to another prisoner.

Every seat on the bus, whether in a cage or not, was taken up by the backside of a prisoner. Besides the full restraints, prisoners were shackled to each other in groups of four, just in case any inmate harbored thoughts about overpowering the three armed guards on board and making a run for it. Actually, any escape plan would have been a suicide mission because one of the guards sat in his own cage at the rear of the bus, his fingers poised on the trigger of a 12-gauge shotgun that poked through a metal opening.

We rolled out of Delano a little after 5:00 a.m., still dark as night. Except for the occasional cough or the revving of the diesel engine, the prison bus was as silent as a tomb. The prisoners had heard the message loud and clear from the gruff guards: *sit straight, shut up, and make this easy on both sides.*

Inside the Gray Goose, I tried to move my legs, which were so constricted that my kneecaps butted up against the wire mesh wall in front of me. I felt claustrophobic perched in that dinky enclosure—like I was sitting in an old phone booth. I knew the guards wouldn't have been sympathetic if I complained about the cramped conditions. I was just thankful I wasn't tall, big, or fat. Otherwise, I'd have been in a heap of hurt. As it was, I was extremely uncomfortable.

✦ ✦ ✦

While rambling north on Highway 99, I stared at passenger cars passing by. Occasionally I saw elementary-age kids plant their impressionable faces against their windows and look up at the Gray Goose in fascination. They probably wondered who the boogey men were behind the darkened glass.

The Gray Goose was full for its flight north. A sack lunch and the snacks I brought helped pass the time. About four hours later, we pulled into Jamestown, an hour east of Modesto. Jamestown was the location of the Sierra Conservation Center, which doesn't sound like a state prison but certainly was a correctional facility. Tucked up against the base of the Sierra Nevada mountains, the sprawling Sierra Conservation Center was called Jamestown by the prison population.

Jamestown had another nickname—Camp Snoopy. This minimum-to-medium security prison allowed certain low-risk inmates to escape barb wire fences by volunteering to fight forest fires in the great outdoors. An opportunity to play Smokey the Bear wasn't going to happen for me, however.

The bus nearly emptied out when we stopped at Jamestown and took on more prisoners in transit. I had to stay on the Gray Goose for the entire stop—and try to not think about peeing. After a half hour, we resumed our journey to Sacramento and New Folsom Prison, arriving in two hours. In all, I traveled 267 miles between Delano to New Folsom without a bathroom break. Sitting seven hours in a cage was a *long* time.

The approach into new surroundings took my mind off the urge to urinate. My first and lasting impression about New Folsom was the height of the concrete walls surrounding the one-hundred-acre prison grounds that lay in the shadow of Folsom Dam. Those walls had to be three stories high and were made of smooth concrete. Catwalks overlooked the exercise yards. I saw guards pacing on the catwalks, their arms cradling Mini-14s—small, lightweight semi-automatic rifles not known for their accuracy. Then again, they would be shooting fish in a barrel, so hit or miss, they would be firing close enough to get everyone's attention.

When the Gray Goose pulled into one of the walled-off sections, we were greeted by two dozen prison guards decked out in riot gear—body and shoulder protectors, kneepads, shin guards, polycarbonate helmets, face shields, black batons, Tasers, and pepper spray. The show of force was over the top and a reminder that life would be different in this prison.

The handful of prisoners who made the trip from Delano and Jamestown exited the bus in single file, hands clasped in front and held in place by waist chains. There was a welcoming committee, although I didn't see any tea and cookies set out on a silver platter.

* * *

The warden, dressed in a conservative coat and tie and standing next to a phalanx of serious-looking guards, cleared his throat. "Welcome to New Folsom State Prison," he began, using the unofficial name. "Here are my rules. The first one is that this is my prison. You will do what I say because we own this property," he said, nodding to the correctional officers dressed in riot gear and the guards perched on the outer wall with rifles trained on us.

"Some of you will die because of your sentence in this prison," he continued in a straight-talk manner. "Some of you will die in this prison because you're stupid. If that happens, and you're murdered in my prison and no one claims your body, New Folsom State Prison will do the honors and you will be buried by your peers inside these walls as we have the only prison cemetery in the State of California."

That was comforting to know.

The warden was just getting warmed up. "I want you to look at the wall to your right. Do you see that sign?"

My eyes landed on a white sign with red lettering that said: No Warning Shots Fired in This Yard.

"You'll notice that there will be absolutely no warning shots fired by my guards. In case of a riot, we will not be aiming at your feet, we will not be aiming at your legs, and we will not be aiming at your torso. We will be aiming directly at your heads to kill you."

With the end of that cheery pep talk, the warden issued a chipper

"Welcome, and enjoy your stay" salutation, turned on his heels, and left the yard.

When the warden was gone, a guard approached me with a manila file in his hand. "Diaz, follow me," he ordered.

I was led inside the prison to an interview room of sorts—and thankfully given a chance to relieve myself. Afterward, the guard introduced himself as a gang coordinator and got right down to business.

"Listen closely, Diaz, so I don't have to repeat this. We know who you are. We know that you're a banger and a shot caller, and we're watching you. If we hear of any gang activity while you're in here, we'll make sure that you will spend the rest of your sentence in a SHU, in solitary. I'm talking Level IV the entire way. Trust me, you won't want to spend any more time in here than you have to. Any crime that is committed can and will be prosecuted to the full extent of the law, and you'll end up in a bigger jam than ever before."

My response to this bluster? A wry smirk. What were they going to do to me? Lock me up? I was already incarcerated for the next ten years.

◆ ◆ ◆

Like a scarlet letter, my red jumpsuit symbolized my "shot caller" status, which was confirmed in the file held by the gang coordinator.

I didn't keep the red jumpsuit for very long, though. Upon my arrival at New Folsom, I had to return the red jumpsuit and wear what the guards gave me, which wasn't much: a white T-shirt, white boxers, a set of socks, and a pair of shower shoes. I also received one bed sheet, one thin gray blanket, a tiny tube of toothpaste, and the shortest toothbrush you ever saw in your life. You'll notice that I wasn't given any pants or shorts, which means all I had to wear around my waist were my briefs. Another indignity was not having a pillow, so I didn't have anything to place beneath my neck when I tried to sleep.

This was the treatment that Level IV prisoners in solitary confinement received. Why did I receive that classification?

The state prison system classifies prisoners based on their crimes and length of sentence, past gang affiliation, and risk to society. Each state prison is designed to house inmates who are given a security level ranging from Level I to Level IV. The higher the level, the more dangerous the inmate.

The security levels are as follows:

- Level I: open dormitories without a secure perimeter
- Level II: open dormitories with secure perimeter fences and armed guards
- Level III: individual cell, fenced perimeters, and armed guards
- Level IV: cells, fenced or walled perimeters, electronic security, and more staff and armed officers both inside and outside the facility

Within Level IV are Security Housing Units (SHU), which are the most secure areas within the prison and provide maximum coverage. According to the California Department of Corrections and Rehabilitation, SHUs are "designed to handle inmates who cannot be housed with the general prison population, and this includes inmates who are validated gang bosses, prison gang members, or shot callers."

That would be me. I figured that somewhere along the line my shot-caller status was either evident or revealed by a snitch.

I was well aware that a SHU was prison shorthand for solitary confinement. I would not be sharing a cell with one, two, or three other prisoners, nor would I be housed in a dorm-style environment like I was at Wayside. Instead, I would be cooped up in an eight-by-ten-foot windowless cell with a steel-cased door known as a "gate." I would eat all my meals inside my cell with my food slipped through a slot in the steel door. Visits with family and friends would be strictly no contact; I would be on one side of a glass partition, speaking on a phone to a visitor on the other side. Social interactions with other inmates would be nonexistent or severely limited at best. Ditto for the guards.

I had had some experience with solitary confinement in the past two years, but I was still shocked by the "nothingness" of my cell when I was led inside for the first time. My eighty-square-foot cell, outlined with concrete walls painted in a yellowish beige, came with a single bed and a toilet with a sink above it.

Since I had no windows and thus no daylight, my cell was dimly illuminated by a heavy Plexiglas light in the ceiling that couldn't be turned off. This meant that I had to sleep—or at least try to—with a light on the entire time. Further compounding my disorientation was having no clock or wristwatch inside the cell, which meant that I had trouble distinguishing whether it was day or night or what time it was. Only the arrival of my meals around 5:00 a.m., 11:00 a.m., and 5:00 p.m. gave me any sense of what time it might be.

There wasn't anything inside my prison cell except what I have described so far. No TV, no radio, and certainly no computer. Reading books isn't often denied prisoners, but for some reason, I was not allowed to receive any books from the prison library.

Add this all up, and what it meant was that I had literally nothing to do for twenty-three hours a day. Talk about sensory deprivation.

I had been told by prisoners in Wayside and Delano that if you're not strong-minded and strong-willed, then solitary confinement could absolutely break you.

That would not happen to me, but there were times when I wondered if I would be able to keep my sanity.

chapter nine

DUCKS IN A ROW

I arrived at New Folsom sometime in November 1987, just as the weather was turning cold. There was no heating in my cell—or air conditioning. All I had to wear were boxers and a T shirt.

What happened when it got cold in the cell? Tough luck. I performed calisthenics—jumping jacks, push-ups, and leg lunges—to warm up my body. When it got really cold, I wrapped my thin blanket around my shoulders and paced my cell. That's all I could do.

When summer came around, the cell turned into a Swedish sauna. At night, it was so uncomfortable to sleep that there were times when I flooded my sink and splashed water around the cell. Then I slept on the wet floor until the water dried up—at which time I'd splash more water on the floor to stay cool.

Dealing with the hot and cold were nothing compared to the mental challenge of rarely interacting with another live human being. Generally speaking, the only human contact I had was when a guard escorted me to a recreation room for my daily sixty-minute exercise period or to the showers, where I was allowed to bathe three times a week. Each time I left my cell, I wore handcuffs attached to a waist chain.

The rec room felt more like a bigger cell and had twenty-foot-high cement walls. My handcuffs were removed, but my waist chain was attached to a nearby wall, so I didn't have that much freedom. This was a solitary experience as well. I could play handball against myself, smacking a small blue ball with either hand against a wall, or I could shoot baskets at a basketball hoop. My only other exercise option was to do pull-ups on a bar.

As for my personal hygiene, my handcuffs were also taken off when I showered, but I was chained to a bar in the shower stall as a security precaution. At least my hands were free to turn on the shower spray to the right temperature. I was also allowed to remove my T-shirt and boxers, which gave me an opportunity to wash them.

If you're thinking that prisoners handed in their boxers and T-shirts each week for new ones, you would be wrong. I was told that those would be the only undergarments I would receive . . . and I ended up wearing the same underwear and T-shirt for a long time. There was no Macy's inside the SHU.

Showers were limited to five minutes . . . and sometimes stretched to ten minutes if the guards were in a good mood. I used a towel to dry off myself and twisted my wet clothes as much as I could to get the water out. Let's face it: I still trudged back to my cell in wet boxers and T-shirt.

Another huge adjustment to life in solitary confinement was the absolute and never-ending boredom. Being cooped up in a small cell for twenty-three hours a day with nothing to do meant looking for ways to keep my mind engaged.

I'd sit on my bed and count the holes in the ceiling. They were very tiny holes, but that was part of the challenge. (I still remember the exact number: 3,680.) I'd unroll my toilet paper and tally the sheets—and carefully roll the toilet paper back up. Then I'd study the slot in my cell door—which was used to deliver my food tray—and imagine a factory worker manufacturing the cell door or producing the slot's frame in a blue-collar setting.

A small milk carton set on each food tray provided a lot of entertainment. The logo on the carton said PIA Milk, which meant the dairy product came from the Prison Industry Authority. New Folsom had a farm on prison grounds with a herd of cows that were looked after and milked by Level I and Level II inmates.

I'd count the number of words on the carton, then the number of letters, the number of vowels, the number of consonants . . . and then look at the words and wonder if there was another word that could be made from the letters. For instance, *milk* couldn't be made into another word, but *prison* could be turned into *porsin* or *ropsin*. I had no idea if those were actual words, but I imagined they were and made up definitions.

Origami—the Japanese art of folding paper into decorative shapes and figures—was another way I used my imagination and kept my mind occupied. I read a book about origami in juvenile hall, so I understood the basics of creating new forms out of paper. While in solitary confinement, I spent hours refashioning a milk carton into a bird of prey, a house on the street, or a flying machine that would stay in the air when launched from my bed.

Solitary confinement, I would learn, was one of the most brutal punishments that man can inflict on man. The extreme-but-not-total absence of human interaction—talking, touching, or seeing another human face—really took some getting used to. In a Level IV solitary housing unit situation, prisoners had very little to absolutely no communication with other inmates. Whoever designed the SHU system made sure that the minimal contact with guards remained as impersonal as possible.

Here's what I mean. Each time a guard opened my slot to give me my food, the only thing I could see through the slot were the guard's boots and the top of his ankles. My three-times-a-day meal deliveries were the only time I actually "saw" another human being while I was inside my cell—if you count seeing a guard's uniform and work boots as human contact. The slot was positioned in the gate in such a way that I could never see a face or make eye contact—unless the guard got in a catcher's crouch.

The only way I kept time was by my mealtimes. My first meal of the day arrived around 5:00 a.m., which is how I knew a new day was starting. The prison food was horrible. I realize no one will shed tears on my behalf, but whatever was slid through the slot was guaranteed to look like crap.

Let's just say that the prison staple known as "@#$% on a shingle"—some kind of mystery meat swimming in gag-producing sauce and slapped on a piece of half-toasted white bread—would have been like eating at the Ritz. The slop we were served came from a bunch of leftovers—a mixture of potatoes, broccoli, carrots, and the mystery meat of the day—that were thrown together in an industrial mixer, made into a ball, half heated up, and served cold. Lunch and dinner were more of the same: Wonder bread sandwiches filled with liquid mixes of who-knows-what and dinky portions of gray meat served with undercooked potatoes.

The only thing I looked forward to on my plate was my carton of PIA milk, which I used to amuse me for the rest of the morning until the next meal was left in the slot.

✦   ✦   ✦

Studying the carton of PIA milk was something I did to keep my mind active. I had heard that many of the guys in solitary confinement start hearing voices, start talking to themselves, and lose their minds within weeks of arriving. They can't handle the solitude so they become suicidal.

It wasn't long before I heard disturbing sounds or overheard unsettling conversations outside my cell. I heard guys slamming their heads against the cement walls with such force that there was a sickening thud, followed by the yelling of guards as they carted off the prisoner to the infirmary. Other prisoners ran headlong into their prison door and slammed their faces against the gate. That's solid metal, and hearing them bust their heads was awful.

The prisoner next door to me was called Piggy. I'm not sure why he had that nickname. Since our cells were at the end of the SHU, we could talk to each other through our gate slots since the guards couldn't hear us talking.

Piggy, I learned, was convinced that he had a bunch of ducks in his cell, which was comical and extremely sad. Whenever he left his cell for exercise or a shower, I opened my slot and listened to his interaction with the guard. Most of the time, Piggy didn't want to leave until all his ducks left with him. He insisted to the guard that one of his ducks was still in his cell.

"I'm not going anywhere until I have all my ducks," he would say.

"Piggy, you ain't got no ducks," the guard would reply. "Get a move on."

"I'm not going anywhere until you get my missing duck."

And around and around it would go.

If Piggy let it go, the incident passed. If he didn't, he was carted off to the pysch ward and placed in a rubber room with a straitjacket. A few days or a few weeks later, Piggy would be returned to the cell next to mine.

I heard snippets of other prisoners completely losing it inside the SHU. I'm talking about people peeing on themselves inside the cell, throwing fecal matter at the guards, screaming at the top of their lungs until forcibly stopped, or babbling like village idiots.

The only thing that kept me halfway sane was the hope that I could someday become "mainline" and join the rest of the prison population. This would entail a transfer to a Level IV lockup—known as a "4 yard," where I'd have a lot more interaction with other prisoners. But in order to do that, I'd have to "de-program," meaning I'd have to prove that I didn't want any part of the gang culture.

Even though my shot-caller status meant nothing inside New Folsom, that was my identity. I wasn't quite ready to give up on that, so I decided that I would do my time and let it go.

◆　◆　◆

After a year or so at New Folsom, I heard the guards come by my cell with an announcement: "Protestant service, Protestant service. Any inmate wanting to go the Protestant service, stand by your gate."

I had heard the same announcement for Catholics. Religion wasn't something I was interested in. I had been baptized a Catholic when I was an infant, but that was as far as "religion" went in my life. The last occasion I was inside a church was the time I made my First Communion when I was seven years old. I knew next to nothing about God or Jesus Christ except that He was the one who was on all those crucifixes. I wasn't sure why that happened, but I didn't care.

I didn't even know who Protestants were, what they did, or what they believed. I certainly wasn't interested in going to one of their services, even if that meant an opportunity to leave my cell. I never paid attention to the guards' call for the Protestant service.

One time I was lying on my bed, listening to the voices outside. There seemed to be a few. I imagined what they looked like as a way to keep my mind engaged. I heard an older woman say, "Is that a cell there?"

My cell was at the far end, tucked in a corner and away from the other cells and the guard's post.

"Yes, ma'am, that's a cell, but you don't want to deal with that person," the guard said.

At the time, I wasn't sure if the guard was talking about me. He probably was, but it didn't matter. I shrugged off the conversation anyway.

A week later, I heard the older woman again. She sounded Southern and spoke with a syrupy drawl. "Is there someone in that cell?" she repeated.

"You can go ahead and approach the cell, but I'm letting you know that Diaz is in there. You're wasting your time." The guard spoke directly.

"Well, I'd like to go ahead and approach his cell. Jesus came for him too."

That's when I knew they were talking about me. I figured that lady was just as nuts as some of the inmates banging their heads against the concrete.

She approached the cell. "Young man, can I speak with you?"

I looked through the open slot in my gate. I couldn't see anything except for the guard's boots and a pair of spindly legs. Her skin tone confirmed the accent in her voice: she was African American. From the length of her legs, she had to be short.

"How are you doing?" she asked.

"I couldn't be better," I replied sarcastically.

"I'd like to invite you to our Bible study. I think that it would be something you'd enjoy."

"I don't think that's for me." I had no idea what a Bible study was, but it sure sounded weird.

"If you come, at least you're outside of your cell for an extra hour. We'd love to have you join us."

She had a point there.

"I'm good," I said, which was another way of saying no.

"Young man, I'm going to pray for you. But there's something else I want to tell you: Jesus is going to use you."

That statement confirmed that this lady was crazy. Jesus was going to use me? How was that going to happen? Couldn't she see that I had been thrown into solitary confinement with the lock and key thrown away?

"I don't think that's going to happen," I said.

"Young man, every time I'm here, I'm going to come by and I'm going to invite you to our Bible study. And Jesus is going to use you."

Yeah, right. What an outlandish thing to say.

I was flat-out uninterested in religion in general and Christianity in particular. I couldn't wrap my head around what she was saying. Nothing she said made sense to me.

But true to her word, this little old lady came by my cell once a month. Each time she said two things:

"I'm praying for you, and Jesus is going to use you."

chapter ten

WRITING AND RECEIVING

Prisoners in the SHU were allowed to receive mail and write letters—as many as we wanted.

Well, we weren't really allowed to receive letters because we were not permitted to touch any incoming mail. The way they did things in the SHU, the prison authorities opened your mail and made transparencies of your letters, which they showed you by means of an overhead projector parked outside your cell door that projected your letters through the open slot onto the back wall of your cell. And that's how you read your mail.

If you wanted to *write* a letter, the guards gave you a tiny pencil, just two inches long—barely long enough to hold in your fingers—as well as state-issued yellow paper and a state-issued stamped envelope.

I didn't write or receive too many letters for two reasons:

- I wasn't fond of writing.
- There were only two people who wrote me—my mother and my girlfriend, Camila, whom I met at Mount Vernon Junior High.

Camila was a girl my age who was part of the Drifters gang. What many people don't know is that many gangs are co-ed. There were girls in the hood who were attracted to guy gang members in the same way that groupies are drawn to rock stars and big-time athletes. For the guys, having girls around meant there were cute things to mess with, so it was a two-way street. They wanted to hook up with us, and we wanted to hook up with them.

Don't think that girls hung around male-dominated gangs solely to provide sexual favors or be eye candy, however. I knew plenty of girl gang members who had no problem joining us on home invasions and duct-taping frightened victims while we ransacked homes. I also knew a few girls who killed other gang members when ordered to settle a score.

Camila wasn't the violent type. She was well-spoken, very pretty, and didn't dress like girl gangbangers, so she wasn't slutty in appearance. There was something different about her, which is why I liked her so much. In fact, I put her on such a pedestal that I never had sex with her. It wasn't because I was sexually inexperienced—I had lost my virginity when I was thirteen—but Camila was that special to me, so I treated her accordingly. I remained loyal to her from the time I met her at age fourteen until I was put away at age sixteen.

Camila was a regular visitor on Sunday afternoons when I was at Men's Central Jail in downtown LA while I was being tried for second-degree murder and armed robbery. After I was sentenced, she would drive my mother nearly two hours to see me in the East Max wing at Wayside, north of Los Angeles. After I caught a chain to New Folsom and was put in solitary four hundred miles north of Los Angeles, she wrote me regularly.

At first I enjoyed her letters; she was my only contact with the outside world, except for my mother. She described how she decided to leave the gang lifestyle after being accepted by Job Corps, a federal program administered by the US Department of Labor that provided vocational and academic training for at-risk youth. Young men and women received room and board while they were part of Job Corps.

I was pleased that Camila was trying to build a better life for herself. Then, after I was in the SHU for a couple of years, she wrote that she had moved to Ogden, Utah, and was studying to become a nurse. As part of her training, she was working in a hospital.

Camila kept saying in her letters that she was waiting for me, that she was saving a place in her heart for me, but reading those words gave me heartache. After two years in the SHU, I still had at least another six years of solitary confinement ahead of me. Even I could see that she needed to be free to pursue her dreams. There was no future for us.

"I think it's best you stop writing me," I wrote in pencil one time. "You've got a great head on your shoulders and you've left your past. You're working in a hospital. You could easily end up dating some doctor or someone in the medical field. You can make something with your life."

Camila wrote me back a book—sixteen pages of lovesick prose. But in my heart, I knew I needed to cut things off and stop wasting her time. I wrote her a short letter and thanked her for knowing me but reminded her that she needed to move on. I ended my letter by saying, "Please don't contact me again." Our break needed to be total.

What I did was unusual for prisoners. When I was at Wayside, I knew guys who were writing ten to fifteen women, milking them for visits, money, and receiving packages filled with toiletries. Later, when I arrived at New Folsom, inmates were allowed to receive Levi's jeans, nice white Stafford T-shirts, and white socks and underwear from the outside, so many prisoners wrote their "girlfriends" and asked them to send clothes or money for the commissary, where they could purchase hygiene items, snacks, drinks, and radios.

I couldn't do that. I decided that I didn't want to be involved with anyone on the outside, except for my mother. Girlfriends like Camila needed to be cut from my life, so that's what I did.

Camila sent me a couple more letters, which I ignored. Her last attempt at communication was an Easter card that said, "I hope you're doing well. I miss you."

I had no idea what "Easter" meant, but that was beside the point. I didn't write her back, and I never heard from her again.

And that was good for the both of us.

◆　◆　◆

Three years into solitary confinement, I really wondered if I could handle seven more years of limited contact with other human beings. Staying sane was a challenge.

I heard prisoners yelling from their cells and acting crazy, which prompted heavy-handed responses from the guards. One of the prisoners making a scene was Demetrius, who was locked up in a cell across from me and closer to the guard station. He was a Crip, a member of one of the biggest black gangs in LA. Everyone knew about the gang rivalry between the Bloods and the Crips and the blood they shed.

The first time I ran into Demetrius was at Camp Miller—the juvenile lock-down near Malibu. I did time with him at East Lake Juvenile Hall and Sylmar Juvenile Hall. After I got sentenced, we were together at 2400 East Max, although my bunk was at one end of the hall with other Latinos and he was at the other end with black gang members.

One time he picked a fight with an older black guy in his midforties. Since this older man was incarcerated at Wayside, he had to have committed a serious offense. Because of his age, it was doubtful that this older man had any gang ties.

As tension escalated while the two men circled each other with their dukes up, every prisoner hustled to one end of the dorm to see what was going on. That included me.

The two black men squared off like they were in a Las Vegas boxing ring, feigning punches. Demetrius taunted his older rival, describing how he was going to kick his @#$% and beat him to a pulp. The insults prompted the elder man to say, "I've had enough of your mouth."

At that moment, the older man took a huge swing at Demetrius, who didn't duck in time. The older man's fist crashed into the side of Demetrius's face, causing his legs to buckle. His eyes rolled back in his head as he struggled to remain upright. Demetrius had really been tagged.

Before Demetrius could find his equilibrium, the older guy clocked him again. This time the blow sent Demetrius to his knees, which caused an uproar in the dorm. In the pandemonium, one of the Crips yelled, "We can't let the homeboys down. This is the Crips."

In other words, since the older black man didn't belong to their gang, he was going to pay. In short order, four Crips mauled the older man and gave him a severe beating.

That was our history when I learned Demetrius was in the SHU with me. He did not adjust well to solitary confinement. One day, he decided that he couldn't take it any longer and went bananas. He spread his own feces across his chest and threw pieces at the guards who came in to restrain him.

I heard him yelling and screaming as he was dragged away. I knew where they were taking him—the psych ward, or more specifically, a rubber room deep inside the psych ward. He didn't return to the SHU for four or five months.

✦ ✦ ✦

I knew other inmates inside the SHU from having served time with them in LA. The reason I knew they were there was because everyone's name was put outside his door, which I'd see on my way to the showers or to my exercise hour.

I remembered them by their clever nicknames—guys like Creeper, a Puerto Rican guy I liked. There was Mugsy, a Korean guy who belonged to the Sureños, a gang in the Echo Park area close to downtown LA. (A lot of Asians were joining Hispanic gangs in those days.) Mugsy and I met at East Max and became good friends. He even met Camila during one of the visitations and was impressed.

"Hey, man, that's your girl?" he said after we got back to the dorm.

"Yeah."

"Man, she's hot."

"Yeah, yeah."

Our conversations were deep.

Later on, Mugsy tried to set me up with his sister before I caught a chain to New Folsom. She wanted to see me at Wayside, but I denied the visit. Like I said, I was loyal to Camila when we were an item.

Not long after I broke things off with Camila, I was nearing the end of my third year inside the SHU. I think. You can never be too sure in an environment where there are no clocks and the dim light in your cell never goes off.

Three years—more than a thousand days—was a long, long time. Piggy had been there ten years when I arrived, so I totally understood why he was certain there were ducks in his cell. While many prisoners in the SHU knew they would get out sometime, there were some guys with indefinite sentences, meaning they were never getting out. I don't know how they mentally handled that.

As for me, I knew I would serve the rest of my twelve-year, eight-month sentence in solitary confinement. That meant I had at least seven years to go, which was a long time to get my head around.

Knowing that, I concentrated on getting through solitary one day at a time, just like every other prisoner in the SHU. Perhaps that's why a handful of prisoners attended the Protestant or Catholic services that were periodically available. Maybe that helped them do the time, but I wasn't interested.

◆　◆　◆

Once a month, though, I could count on the African American lady with the syrupy drawl approaching my gate. "Darwin," she said, dropping the *r* and pronouncing my name *Dah-win*, "Ah've been praying for yew since I last came here. I believe God is going to yoose you in a mighty way."

She evidently saw my full name posted on the wall outside my cell. Once again, I replied, "I don't think that's going to happen."

She was never deterred. "Jesus loves you so much. It may be difficult to believe that, but He promises to forgive us for every wrong we have done and provide us eternal life if only we will believe in Him. Ask Jesus to reveal Himself to you, and I will continue to pray for you, Dah-win."

And then she was gone.

◆　◆　◆

After establishing that I was a model prisoner, I was allowed to have books. Once or twice a week, a guard wheeled a cart with a stack of books. If you liked a certain author, you could request books from the prison library. I read a few books by Stephen King, including *Different Seasons*, which contained the short story the movie *The Shawshank Redemption* was based on. It told the story of Andy Dufresne, a banker sentenced to life in Shawshank State Penitentiary for murdering his wife and her lover—a crime of passion.

Imprisoned Andy Dufresne writes an author a fan letter, and the author was touched enough that he sent a box of his books to the prison library. Later, when novelist Dean Koontz became my favorite author,

I thought, *What if I wrote Dean Koontz and told him how much I enjoyed his suspense thrillers?*

That's what I did, and I was thrilled when Dean Koontz mailed four boxes of his books to New Folsom, including a box autographed to me. "Thank you for contacting me," he wrote. "I'm pleased that you're enjoying my books and sharing them with other prisoners. Here's a gift for you and the men in your cell block, so please enjoy my entire collection of books."

I also remember another book I picked off the cart because I liked the cover, which showed a well-dressed man in a moustache—who was white—standing outside a prison. The book was entitled *Where Flies Don't Land*, and author Jerry Graham told his story about being part of an Italian/Puerto Rican gang in New York City, doing hits for the mob's five families.

Then Jerry was shot and left for dead by Colombian hit men, but he crawled into a dumpster and escaped certain death. Graham couldn't escape prison, however, and he ended up in a hellhole so bad that not even the flies would land on their prison chow.

Graham's descriptions of prison life fascinated me. At the end of the book, he recounted his conversion experience through the power of Jesus Christ. That part flew over my head at the time.

❖ ❖ ❖

Or did it?

The reason I say this is because several months later, maybe an entire year, I was lying down in my cell. It was midmorning, sometime before lunch. I was daydreaming—about what, I forget—when I turned my head toward the wall opposite my bed.

On that wall, a movie was playing—a movie about my life. I saw myself as a young child, walking the old neighborhood at 9th and Kenmore. Next, I was inside our old apartment, and I saw Dad hitting my mom again. I witnessed incidents from the schoolyard, my early days with the gang—everything in picture-perfect detail. There were scenes that only I would know and remember, and this movie of my life was showing on my cell wall in vivid color—as if there were a movie projector next to my bed.

Except there was no movie projector.

This was weird. Really weird. I was wide awake. I wasn't doped up, and I was in my five senses, but what I was seeing was my entire life story from when I was a young child.

I wondered if I was going nuts like Piggy and his ducks. Maybe my grasp on reality was slipping rapidly.

You're losing your marbles. There's no way I could be seeing these scenes from my past life like I was watching a private movie in my prison cell.

Then I saw a bearded man with long hair carrying a cross. I saw a mob of angry people shouting at this man trudging alone with a cross over his shoulder. The mob looked like they wanted to destroy this guy. From time to time, as he was carrying this cross, I couldn't see his face, but I knew this person carrying the cross was absolutely watching me. He was looking at me despite the fact that I couldn't see his face.

It's hard to describe how this went down, but then he disappeared, and the film resumed showing scenes in real life that actually took place, including stabbings, home invasions, and ransacking other people's stuff. I saw times that I tied up people scared out of their wits and took their wallets with no hesitation. Every event on screen happened exactly the way it happened in real life.

And then the "movie" stopped, and I saw the guy carrying a cross again. People were still screaming at him and had to be held back from getting their hands on this guy.

Once again, I couldn't see his face, but I know he was looking at me. And then he arrived on top of a knoll, where rough-looking men nailed his hands and feet to the wooden cross and raised the cross so it stood between two men, each on crosses of their own. This man was suspended between the sky and the ground.

I didn't understand what was going on. All I knew was that I must be going nuts. What got to me was when this person being crucified looked at me and said, *"Darwin, I'm doing this for you."*

I shuddered. No one knew my real name. Of course, the guards did and so did my family, but nobody at New Folsom called me by my given name. Everyone called me Casey. Yet here was this man on a cross saying, "Darwin, I'm doing this for you."

And then I heard the sound of breath leaving him. At that moment, I knew he died.

That's when I hit the floor in the middle of the cell. I started weeping because I knew somehow that this was almighty God. I knew what I saw even though I didn't understand what he had done for me or what was happening. I just knew that God was trying to get my attention.

After hitting the floor, I knew I had to get on my knees. It felt right. I started confessing my sins.

God, I'm sorry for stabbing so many people.

God, I'm sorry I robbed so many families.

God, I'm sorry for stabbing that gang member in the eye.

God, I'm sorry for beating up that kid outside of school.

I went into full detail and expressed remorse for a long list of transgressions and horrific acts. And each time I confessed something I had done, I felt like another weight came off my shoulders.

And then I made a promise to God: *I will not put my hands on another man again because I know what my hands are capable of—killing another person.*

When I finished, I knew something major had definitely happened.

✦　✦　✦

Several days passed by. I was in my cell. Then I heard God speaking to me: *Go to your gate, knock on it, and ask for a chaplain.*

I didn't know what a chaplain was. I had no clue what a chaplain did. I had never heard the word.

But I definitely discerned correctly, so I got up and knocked on my gate. Sure enough, there was a CO—a correctional officer—walking down the hallway. He stopped.

"Yeah, Diaz?"

"Hey, I'm supposed to talk to the chaplain."

There was an awkward pause. "Are you @#$% me?"

"Nah, man. I'm just supposed to ask you for a chaplain, whatever that is."

"You can't be serious."

"I am. I'm just letting you know that's what I'm supposed to do."

"Give me a minute."

"Take your time."

The CO returned with a request slip and a two-inch pencil. "Fill that out, and give it back to me."

He waited while I filled out my request to see a chaplain.

"I thought I'd seen everything," he mumbled as he walked away.

The next day, three COs came to my cell. They followed the standard protocol when opening my gate, which meant that I had to step to the back of the cell, get on my knees, cross my legs, and raise my hands behind my head with interlaced fingers. Then I was shackled with belly chains and cuffs that restricted my arm movement to the point where I couldn't scratch my nose.

The COs then walked me down a corridor and brought me to a room where a white guy dressed in civilian clothes was waiting for me. We shook hands while he introduced himself as the prison chaplain.

"What's going on?" he asked.

"I'm about to share something with you because God told me that I need to see a chaplain. I guess that's apparently who you are."

"Yes."

"Something happened in my cell a couple of days ago. I didn't go crazy, but this is what I saw with my very own eyes."

I took my time explaining the "movie" that I saw on my cell wall, leaving out no details. When I described how the man looked at me and said, "Darwin, I'm doing this for you," the chaplain's lips quivered, and his eyes turned bloodshot red. He was crying. Seeing his tears caused me to cry because I was remembering what took place.

The chaplain composed himself and exhaled. "That's quite a story," he said. Then he reached for a Bible and flipped through the pages until he found the place he wanted to be. "I'd like to read to you the crucifixion story," he said.

For the next ten minutes or so, I listened to him read from the Bible about how Jesus Christ was betrayed by one of His followers named Judas, arrested by Jewish leaders on charges of blasphemy— whatever that meant—and brought before a Roman governor named Pontius Pilate, who wanted to release an innocent man but capitulated to a raucous crowd that yelled, "Crucify Him! May His blood be on us, and on our children!"

Jesus was whipped, mocked, and given a crown of thorns. Then He was forced to carry His cross through the streets of Jerusalem to a place called Golgotha, where His hands and feet were nailed to the cross. For three hours, He hung on that cross until He said, "It is finished" and died.

Listening to the chaplain read the gospel account of the crucifixion was an "Oh, wow" moment for me. That's when it became real. This event actually took place at some point. I was not going nuts.

"God has visited you," the chaplain said. "What happened in that cell is that you were born again. You experienced salvation."

"What's salvation?"

The chaplain took his time explaining to me the concept of salvation, which is that Christ's death on the cross and subsequent resurrection saved me from God's judgment of sin—sin that had separated me from God. Instead of experiencing the consequence of sin, which was death, I had the assurance of knowing that when I died I would have eternal life with Christ.

The chaplain seemed very excited about me. He gave me a Gideon Bible, with the King James translation. This particular Bible consisted of the New Testament and the book of Psalms and the book of Proverbs from the Old Testament.

◆ ◆ ◆

When I returned to my cell, I read that Bible inside and out. If I was awake, I was reading one of the Gospels or one of the Epistles. I went to sleep reading my Bible and when I'd wake up, I'd discover that I'd slept right on top of it.

Every hour I was awake, I was reading that Bible. I'd spend five, six hours reading, then fall asleep, wake up, do some push-ups and calisthenics, and get back to reading from where I left off. I didn't understand half of what I was reading, but that didn't even bother me. Neither did the *thees* and *thous* that sounded so foreign to me. Even though I didn't quite understand the message, I knew that whatever I was reading made me feel good.

Several weeks after I received the Gideon Bible, I stopped reading. I looked around my bare cell, thinking. Then I heard God's voice speak to me. He said, *When you get out of here, you're going to gather your homies together and tell them that you want nothing to do with the gang life anymore because you're a Christian.*

"Okay," I replied. "I will do that."

I took God's direction to mean that I would say that to gang leaders after I got paroled, but that was a long way off because I still had more than seven years left on my sentence.

A few days later, I was in my cell, reading my Bible. Nothing out of the ordinary. Suddenly, and unexpectedly, my gate opened, which had never happened before in that manner.

You have to understand that in the world of incarceration, there is no such protocol. The system is the system. They never break the system. They never open a prisoner's gate until they've come to the wicket and told you to step all the way to the back of the cell, get on your knees, cross your legs, put your hands behind your head, and interlace your fingers. That's how it was done every single time my cell was about to be opened.

For my gate to suddenly open like that didn't totally freak me out, but it was weird. I looked up from my chair and saw the warden and the CO gang coordinator who greeted me when I arrived from Delano, the same two who told me they were going to make sure that I served the rest of my time in the SHU, in solitary.

The warden spoke first. "I don't know why we're doing this, but we're going to put you in mainline," he said.

✦ ✦ ✦

Mainline. That meant I would leave solitary confinement and be transferred to the main prison population to serve the rest of my sentence with other prisoners.

I didn't say anything. I was too stunned to react because this wasn't supposed to happen. I had been thrown in "the hole" and was supposed to stay in solitary for at least seven more years to finish my twelve-year, eight-month sentence.

"When am I going to mainline?" I asked, afraid to get my hopes too high.

"Right now."

There was nothing to pack. I had the clothes on my back, the shortest toothbrush in the world, and my precious Bible. A few minutes later, one of the guards delivered a fresh set of state blue jeans, a white T-shirt, a pair of socks, and sneakers. I changed into the new garb, grabbed my Bible, but left my toothbrush behind.

Within twenty minutes, I was processed into the B yard and a Level IV unit with two dozen men. Two COs escorted me to my new cell, which was empty.

For the moment, I would have a cell to myself.

I looked around at my new home and thought about how much my life had changed in the last half hour. Then I remembered what God had told me: *When you get out of here, you're going to gather your guys together and tell them that you want nothing to do with the gang life anymore because you're a Christian.*

My heart was ready. I knew that declaring I no longer wanted to be a gang member meant that I was forfeiting my life. I was aware of that, but I was ready to do whatever He wanted me to do.

Even if my actions got me killed.

chapter eleven

BACK IN THE YARD

In the early afternoon of my first full day in mainline, I was alone in my cell, reading my Bible, when the exercise bell rang. My gate automatically unlocked, and I was free to walk out to New Folsom's main exercise yard.

I shielded my eyes when I stepped outside—I hadn't been outdoors in three long years, and the afternoon sun was incredibly bright. But this was no time to revel in the warm sunshine of a spring day because what I was about to do would cost me my life. What propelled my steps was the assurance that I was doing what God wanted me to do and going through what He wanted me to go through. Even though I was keenly aware that this was *not* going to be fun, I had zero fear in my heart.

I knew there were eyes on me, and sure enough, a half dozen gang leaders fell in as I made my way deeper into the exercise yard. They followed me to a concrete picnic table, where I hopped up on the tabletop and let them gather around me. As I made eye contact with several of the gang leaders, I remembered what God told me to say when I got out of the SHU.

"Fellas, I'll get to the point. I'm a Christian now, and I don't want to be a part of this anymore," I announced. By *this* I meant the gang lifestyle.

"I feel like I need to tell you this on my first day in mainline, so that there are no rumors," I continued. "You're hearing it from the horse's mouth."

I also acknowledged the consequences of my declaration. "I know it's not going to go good for me, but being a Christian is who I am now, and that's not going to change."

I would say that the general reaction could be summed up in three words: *Are you nuts?*

I remember a couple of shot callers eyeballing each other. I could read their body language like the front page of the *Los Angeles Times*: *He's no longer one of us, so he needs to be taken out.*

In unison, they turned their backs on me and walked away, mumbling among themselves. In prison lingo, leaving a gang made me a "drop out"—and there were severe consequences for doing so. I was shaming my own kind, my own blood.

From that moment on, I knew there was a green light on my life. I'd get shanked, although strangulation was a possibility. Not that I was brave or felt like I was made out of steel or something, but I took the apostle Paul's words in Philippians 1:21 to heart: "to live is Christ and to die is gain."

For the rest of the exercise hour, I sat on the picnic table and watched furtive conversations take place among various sets of prisoners. I knew these gangbangers were talking about what to do with me since I didn't want to be part of them any longer.

When the bell rang signaling that it was time to return to our cells, I didn't look right, left, or over my shoulder as I headed back to my cell. Part of that was because I didn't think I would be killed right away or in broad daylight—there were too many armed guards in the vicinity who might shoot and ask questions later. But I also decided that I would offer no resistance when my time came. I just wanted the dudes to do it, pinch it off, and go. I wouldn't even look at the people killing me because I didn't want them to feel guilty about what they were doing. Truth be told, I was just as much a scumbag as the next guy in B yard.

I returned to my cell without incident, and my gate closed automatically. I was safe until the next chow call because the best time to do these types of hits was when my cell door racked open just before mealtimes. Another gang member would slip out of his cell like a ghost and stick me with a shank over and over until I bled to death. Or, on his signal, he would be joined by accomplices who'd rush into my cell, knock me down, plant a heavy heel in the middle of my back, and strangle me with a homemade garrote until my eyes popped out and I breathed my last.

✦　✦　✦

In a Level IV yard, there were no small timers. It didn't matter if the dude doing the hit or his accomplices were caught. Most were your seasoned gangbangers with life sentences and nothing to lose. If they were assigned a job by shot callers, they got it done because they *had* to get it done—or face the consequences.

I figured the hit would come either at five o'clock before dinner chow or at six o'clock the following morning before breakfast. Gang leaders don't waste time "taking out the trash," which is what they called killing someone who'd betrayed them.

Suddenly, in the middle of the afternoon, I had a visitor— Mosca, a Latino gangbanger with a normal build, short hair in the back, and a goatee. Sometimes inmates were allowed outside of their cells if they needed to report to a prison job, like working in the laundry room. That would explain why Mosca had the freedom to move about the unit we were in.

I knew Mosca, whose nickname was pronounced *moe-ska* and is Spanish slang for *fly*. He was in the Rockwood gang with me back in LA. When word got around that I didn't want to be part of the gang life any longer, he was likely told to throw out the trash by the shot callers. Their thinking probably went like this: *Your homie turned his back on us. That makes Rockwood responsible for taking him out. You have to clean up your own mess.*

Mosca came up to my gate. "Hey, Casey, you need to change your story because they're asking me to take you out," he said through the wicket.

I wasn't surprised. "Look, I understand the politics in here and that you have to do what you have to do, but I can't change my story," I said. In other words, I wasn't going to renounce my Christianity.

Mosca's nostrils flared in anger. "You don't get it! They're telling me to take you out."

I shook my head. "Sorry, but you don't understand. There's no way I'm changing my story. I know what I saw and who I am now."

I approached my gate and looked Mosca straight in the eyes. "I just want you to know that I forgive you for what you're going to do. It's all good, brother. I forgive you. You need to know that."

Mosca fumed for a moment, then turned on his heels and left my cell door. As he walked away, I knew we were both at a point of no return.

That was a long afternoon, waiting for the call to dinner chow. When my gate opened, though, no one was waiting for me. That astonished me, but then again, the element of surprise is normal in the prison world, just like in the animal world of predator versus prey.

I know it sounds weird to say this, but I wasn't wary or even sick to my stomach. I felt that way because I was immune to the violence.

I walked to the chow hall without incident. I doubted anything would happen inside the prison cafeteria because of the presence of two dozen guards in riot gear standing along the perimeter walls, gripping black batons and ready for action. Backing up the unarmed COs were a trio of "gunners" perched on a catwalk twenty feet above us. They cradled mini-14 semi-automatic assault rifles and meant business. Directly across the catwalk, dozens of bullet holes scarred the concrete walls. The gunners shot to kill, which is why the chow hall wasn't the smartest place to do a single-man hit.

Our unit ate with a half dozen other sections, so there were probably 150 convicts—black, brown, and white—showing up for chow that evening. It's never the same sections eating together two days in a row; the guards do that on purpose, of course, to keep cliques from forming.

My first couple of meals in mainline were sufficient; the food was better than the slop I was served in solitary. The cooks were inmates who took pride in preparing our meals; at breakfast earlier that morning, I actually liked their SOS—@#$% on a shingle—which was gravy with bits of mystery meat served over a homemade biscuit. I washed the SOS down with watered-down coffee.

For my first dinner in mainline, I was served spaghetti with a thin tomato sauce, white bread, and a basic lettuce salad. It wasn't too bad, but I didn't eat with anyone that night. No one was allowed to sit near me.

After finishing my meal, I left the protection of the chow hall and returned to my cell. This time I *was* looking over my shoulder, but nothing happened. When my gate shut behind me, I knew I was safe until breakfast the following morning.

What a restless night! I prayed and read my Bible until dawn, aware that I was going to die. Fear didn't keep me awake, though. I was more curious how the hit would go down: Would it be one guy, like Mosca, sent to stab me, or would several guys pounce on me with shanks or handmade rope? Because I know it's going to happen. It's a rule that it has to happen.

◆　◆　◆

Right around six in the morning, my gate swung open automatically: chow call for breakfast. I was sitting on my bunk bed, reading my Bible. I didn't make a move.

Mosca arrived within seconds. He was alone, which surprised me, but I assumed he told the fellas that he had this and didn't need help.

But then Mosca stopped at the gate door and spoke to me. "You better be right," he said, "because I can't do this to you."

I was puzzled. Usually when you take someone out in a cell, you run in and go to town on him. For Mosca to make a statement before doing what he was going to do was not standard operating procedure. Not only that, he was saying that he couldn't kill me.

Nonetheless, I didn't reply. I guess I didn't believe him. I just looked at Mosca briefly and returned to reading my Bible. Like I said, I wasn't going to put up a fight.

"I can't do this," he repeated. "I just can't."

I decided to get involved. "Look, man. You know there's going to be a green light on *you* if you *don't* do this."

"But Casey, I can't go through with it." Now his lips were quivering. Something had moved in his heart. "You're different. I can tell. Why are you different?"

This was an opening to share my faith.

"Here's what I did, man," I began. "I asked God to forgive me for what I've done. I don't know how all that works out, but look, man, something happened to me back in the SHU. Jesus Christ became real to me. He created the earth and the heavens, and He came on this earth to die on a cross for my sins and yours as well. I don't know what else to tell you except that you need to ask God for forgiveness.

Do that, and He'll forgive you. I'm pretty sure of that. Again, I don't know how it all works, but the question you have to ask yourself is this: Are you ready for what's going to happen to the both of us if you don't take me out? Because we're going to die in here. That's for sure."

Mosca carefully considered my words. After a moment of thought, he said, "I'm down with you." In other words, he was choosing Christ and turning his back on a direct order from the shot callers to take me out.

Nothing more was said between us.

Mosca departed, and word traveled quickly that nothing happened in my cell because there was no blood on him. He didn't do the hit when he had a chance. He messed up, and now two people had to pay the price.

◆　◆　◆

I heard muffled voices in the distance—prisoners talking about what had happened. There was a bad vibe in our unit. I could sense it. I could feel something was wrong and something bad was going to happen. But nothing happened the rest of the day.

The following morning, Mosca and I happened to be in the communal bathroom, brushing our teeth, when a dozen guys jumped us. They knocked us to the ground and started clobbering us. They punched us with their fists and kicked us in the head, neck, arms, torso, and legs. The beating was so horrific that I passed out.

The next thing I knew I woke up in the prison infirmary, black and blue from head to toe. A kind nurse handed me a mirror. I was shocked to see the bumps on my head and black-and-blue contusions and abrasions across my battered face and body.

"That was quite a beating," she said.

I grunted. "Good thing I don't remember anything."

"Yes. You're lucky to still be here."

Instead of trying to kill us, the shot callers decided that Mosca and I would be the recipients of "hard candy"—prison slang for a severe beating. They decided to punish us instead of killing us.

Every few days, at least once a week, we would be in a line movement, going to the head or the showers, and out of nowhere, a dozen guys would jump us. It was almost like a pack of wild coyotes on a toy poodle—and everybody wanted a bite. I usually ended up in the infirmary for a couple of days, but I welcomed that short period of rest. At least I knew I wouldn't get pummeled until I returned to my cell.

Occasionally, a correctional officer would interview me about what happened, but I never gave names. I never pointed anyone out. It wasn't in me to become a snitch.

That was my pride talking. I didn't cooperate because I thought I could handle anything that came my way. After the umpteenth beating, though, a deputy warden offered to put me into a protective custody unit, which prisoners called "junkyards." I was never going to a junkyard, no matter if I got beat up every day of the week and twice on Sunday.

◆ ◆ ◆

One afternoon, I was in my cell after another beating. The pounding wasn't bad enough to send me to the infirmary, but I had my bell rung a few times. To be honest about my feelings, I was angry at God.

I said out loud to Him, "I've given You my life, and this is what I get?"

And then I snapped. I got so mad that I took a Bible and ripped it to shreds. I tore up the Holy Book, ripping pages in half and throwing the cover and bits of paper into the trash can. I flushed the rest down the toilet.

A thought came to my mind. Maybe, just maybe, I needed to break my promise that I would never put my hands on another man.

Maybe I needed to make an example out of one of those dudes who kept jumping me and Mosca. Maybe I should kill one of them, which would send a message to the shot callers.

This was the turmoil I was feeling inside. I was aware that I was living through a dark period.

◆ ◆ ◆

I hadn't heard God's voice for a while, even though I was still reading my Bible for hours a day and participating in several Bible studies. One was led by Abel Ruiz, a former member of Florencia 13, a Los Angeles gang. Four or five inmates joined us for that study. I also attended several Bible studies in the prison chapel led by different prison ministries. My favorite was conducted by a Baptist pastor named Ruben Viveros.

I needed those Bible studies because the persecution was heavy. I was so discouraged, never knowing when I'd get jumped and beaten up again. It's hard to explain this to those who've never been physically assaulted, but it hurts! I didn't have that much meat on my bones, so each punch to my gut and each kick to my arms and legs caused throbbing pain and left me sore for days.

That's why I became unglued in my cell and tore up my Bible in a fit of frenzy. That's why I was thinking of wasting one of my attackers. That's why I had reached my limit. It was time that I looked after Casey Diaz because it was certain that nobody else would.

I decided my first step was to make a shank. I certainly had practice with that art. I took a couple of dull, used razor blades and broke them in a way that I could form a longer blade. Then I melted a plastic toothbrush onto the edge of the razor blades. For a handle, I ripped into my bedsheet and wrapped the cloth around the toothbrush.

And now I had a deadly shank at my disposal.

This is what I was thinking at that moment: *The next guy who comes into my cell to deliver some hard candy, I'm going to put my hand over his face and drive my shank into his neck and keep sawing until I cut off his head. Then I'll drag the rest of his lifeless torso in front of my cell and leave him there for everybody to see. That will make anyone think twice about coming after me.*

At the time, I had been receiving beatings for months. I was getting sick and tired of taking the poundings and not fighting back.

◆　◆　◆

One day I was in my cell. I had hidden my shank inside my mattress. I pulled out my dangerous weapon and looked at it, which caused me to pause. I decided that I needed to fast and pray about the path I was heading down.

For the next two days, I didn't leave my cell for the chow hall. I remained behind and read my Bible. (I had a second Bible left after I destroyed the one Bible.) A verse from Proverbs stood out like it was ringed with neon lights: "For they eat the bread of wickedness, and drink the wine of violence" (4:17 NIV).

I was about to drink the wine of violence, and that meant I was eating the bread of wickedness.

God's Word calmed me down. I came to my senses. I did not want to eat that bread or drink from the cup of violence again.

Suddenly, I had a visitor. My cell door was open for some reason, and standing there was a "lookout" guy—a prisoner in my unit who would signal to a half dozen other homies that the coast was clear to give Casey another helping of hard candy.

But his jaw dropped when he saw the shank in my hand. He bolted and ran away.

I knew then that I had to get rid of my shank. I broke up the crude knife into pieces and flushed them down the toilet—and thanked God that I never got caught with the shank by the authorities.

I also thanked God I wasn't in rage mode because I'm 100 percent sure I would have taken this dude out if he took me on.

◆   ◆   ◆

Not long after I destroyed my shank, I got roughed up again, which was greatly discouraging. A CO dropped by my cage and said there was a lady counselor who wanted to see me. I figured talking to a counselor couldn't hurt, so I agreed to see her.

Two correctional officers escorted me through a series of hallways and past several buzzer gates. Finally, I was ushered into the lady counselor's office. She was looking through my file. I noticed she was wearing a crucifix around her neck and there was a Bible on the corner of her desk.

After asking how I was doing, she said, "It's no secret that you've been getting jumped quite often since you were transferred to the Level IV population. What we've noticed is that you're not defending yourself or helping us nail the perpetrators. In fact, whenever a correctional officer interviews you, you refuse to name names."

I remained quiet and didn't respond. The lady counselor set down her file and took off her glasses.

"Mr. Diaz, we're also aware that you're attending several Bible studies and are taking your Christian faith seriously. You need to know that as a Christian, you have every right to defend yourself. There's nothing wrong with fighting back if someone attacks you, even in here. May I remind you that the majority of the prison population is incarcerated at New Folsom because they committed murder. You never know. You could be next. I think you need to be reminded of this."

"Thank you," I said. "I'll think about what you said."

I mulled over the lady counselor's words for several days, unsure how I should respond to being jumped in the future. But something else was also on my mind: I would be seeing my mother for the first time in three and a half years.

Once I caught a chain to New Folsom, it was impossible for her to visit because she hadn't owned a car in years. Don't forget that my old girlfriend Camila drove her to Men's Central Jail and Wayside to see me before I was transferred to New Folsom.

I never asked my mom to visit me. She didn't have the money to fly to Sacramento, so I didn't want her to feel guilty about not making the effort to see me. But then I heard about a California state program that paid for a special bus to transport inmate families from downtown LA to New Folsom—up and back in the same day.

I told her about the state bus during one of our infrequent phone calls.

"I want to see you," my mother said. "What do I need to do?"

"You have to fill out an application, and then they review it. When you get the okay, you can come and see me."

Several months passed, and then my mom received approval to see me on a certain date. If I had a calendar, I would have circled the date.

When that Sunday arrived, I was allowed to leave my cell and wait in a visitor's room for Mom. I made small talk with other inmates. We swapped stories about the foods our mothers cooked or the special things they did for us. I also passed the time reading my Bible. I wanted to show Mom that I was a Christian.

Suddenly, a side door opened. The state bus had arrived. Several dozen family members walked in, but my mother was not there. I searched every face, but she wasn't on that bus.

It's hard to describe how deflated I felt. Later I learned that something in the paperwork was wrong and she wasn't allowed to board, but at the time, I didn't know that and was really bummed. The only person who cared whether I lived or died in this world hadn't come to see me. My own mother was a no-show. I was absolutely devastated.

I was returned to my unit, Bible in hand. I was nearing my cell when a gangbanger loitering outside his cell stopped me.

"What's up, Bible-thumper?" he sneered.

I made eye contact with this dude. I recognized him as one of the guys who participated in the group beatings. He was always a part of the bunch.

I didn't say anything, but my blood quickly bubbled to a boiling point. I almost made it to my cell, but then I turned back and approached him.

"What did you say?" I asked. My tone was threatening.

"I said, 'What's up, Bible-thumper?' You have a problem with that?"

A smirk lingered on his face. I'll call him Spanky.

"Tell you what," I said. "Why don't you come down to my cell, and if you have anything to get off your chest, we can do it there."

I walked away from Spanky. He didn't follow, which I expected.

An hour or two later, it was dinner time. The gates racked open, and Spanky stuck his head inside my cell and issued a challenge: "You and I are going to meet after chow," he said.

Since Spanky had never taken me on one-on-one, this meant he wanted to meet me with a complement of homies and have them administer another beat-down.

That wasn't going to happen.

I jumped off my bed, snatched him by the neck, pulled him into my cell, and shut my cell door, locking him behind bars. Now it was just him and me. He couldn't get out.

I started mowing this guy down. I went off and released a fury of blows with my clenched fists, one after another, working my arms like pistons. I beat him severely. Then I started slamming his head against the cement walls.

There was blood everywhere in that cell, but I wasn't finished. I banged his face on the floor. I kicked him for good measure. I stomped on top of his head and face.

Then I tried to pick Spanky up. His legs were like gummy worms—no stability. He could barely stand. I pinned him against a wall and looked into his dazed face. One eye went one way and the other eye went another way.

"Next time you think about picking on another Christian in here, I'm going to kill you," I said. "Don't doubt me on this."

I wondered what to do next. Then I looked over at my gate. I thought my cell door was completely locked, but I could see it wasn't closed.

I dragged Spanky and his wobbly legs out of my cell. He didn't know what planet he was on. Spanky had lost complete knowledge of where he was at that moment. There was no doubt that I had given him the beating of his life.

When I tossed him out of my cell, he hit the concrete floor. A black inmate named Rodrigo, who was across from me and to the right, was on his wicket because he could hear the pounding.

"This @#$% doesn't even know where he's at," Rodrigo said.

Spanky was so beat up that he stayed inside the infirmary for three weeks. The guards found out what happened, but they didn't do anything about it. There were no questions asked. Maybe they did nothing because they thought Spanky deserved some hard candy.

As for myself, I knew I had broken my promise to God that I would not lay my hands on anybody again. I felt like a scumbag, even after I confessed what I had done to my Bible study groups, including the one led by Pastor Viveros.

His counsel was something like this: "What you did was wrong because you knew better. You premeditated on this thing, but you know, this is where sinners are saved by grace. These are the mistakes we make, especially in an environment like this. We know you guys have it tough."

Pastor Viveros told me that Jesus still loved me, in spite of ripping up a Bible, in spite of my beat-down to that guy. He took me through the Scriptures and showed me how to ask for forgiveness, which I sought with the Lord.

That still didn't make me feel better. I felt like I screwed up, especially after I was approached by one of the inmates while I was brushing my teeth before lights out.

"Hey, man, what you did with homeboy, you're not supposed to be doing that," he said.

As far as I was concerned, he was not even supposed to be talking to me in the first place. I told him, "Listen, man, I'm done with being nice, as far as that goes. If you bring it to me, I'm going to bring it to you, and if it means I have to stick somebody, then that's what's going to happen. It is what it is."

He looked at me and must have felt the seriousness of my words because he turned and walked away.

I felt bad about threatening him with his life. My pride was getting in the way. *Does it have to come to this point, where I need to do this?*

I pondered those thoughts and prayed for guidance.

I mentioned that I had not been hearing from God like I used to in solitary. But after this unfortunate incident with Spanky, I did hear from Him when I was in my cell. God said to me, *Make it right and ask for his forgiveness.*

✦　✦　✦

At this point, Spanky was back from the infirmary but on bed rest in his cell. He wasn't even coming out. His meals were delivered to him.

One time, when I had freedom of movement, I rolled over there. For some reason, I knew his cell was unlocked, so I opened his gate and walked in. Spanky looked up from his bed and about pooped in his pants. He thought I was coming in there for seconds.

I held my hands up. "Hey, I just want to say that I'm sorry for what I did to you. I shouldn't have done that. It was my fault. I'm really sorry for what I did. I hope it's all good. I want us to get back to a point where you do your thing in here, and I do mine."

Spanky relaxed. "Sure, man," he replied.

Something interesting happened after that. Spanky never looked me in the eye again. When I would walk by him, he would stare at the ground. He never lifted his eyes. Not only that, a lot of the other guys did the same thing.

Looking back, my beat-down of Spanky calmed the situation quite a bit. The beatings of Mosca and me didn't end completely, but they were much more infrequent and not as intense.

And for that, I was thankful to the Lord for His provision, but I still felt like I was being persecuted for my faith. I knew I had to trust in the Lord for my safety as well as the safety of other Christians inside New Folsom.

◆　◆　◆

After a year in mainline, Abel Ruiz and I were inseparable. We always sat together in chow hall, hung out at the same Bible studies, attended the same chapels, and talked about what we were learning in God's Word. We had each other's backs.

One time we were out in the exercise yard when a big race riot started. I don't know who started it, but the Crips and Latino gangs fiercely turned on each other.

The COs responded with brute force, sending in dozens outfitted in riot gear. They swung their black batons left and right, taking down prisoners they passed. Rubber-ball grenades and tear gas canisters rained down on us from guards gathered along on the perimeter of the yard.

Shouts of "Get down!" filled the yard. Abel and I hit the floor. Minutes passed, and when the guards finally got the yard under control, the toxic, pungent smell of tear gas filled the air. People were coughing and sneezing to the point where snot came out of their mouths and noses. The tear gas came on very strong.

While I was lying prostrate on the ground, I saw a boot next to me. Next thing I knew, the CO grabbed me and told me to get up.

I'd been around enough rumbles that I knew the rules: prisoners have to stay on the ground until the COs have full control of everybody. One by one, they use zip ties on everyone. Then you're escorted back to your cell or wherever they deem fit.

Instead, a pair of COs helped Abel Ruiz and me to our feet in the midst of the chaos. "We're getting you out of here," one of the guards said. "We know you had nothing to do with this. We don't want you to smell these fumes."

The fact that we were taken away from the yard before anyone else—without zip ties!—baffled me until I realized the significance of what was happening: God was putting His hand of protection on us in this moment. It was almost like God was saying, *I'm still here.*

But here's where the story gets better. Right after this riot, the warden shipped out every Hispanic gang member from our unit—all of them to different prisons. The only Latinos to stay behind were Abel and myself. Inmates from other prisons and county jails filled the empty cells, but none of them had a history with us.

It was like I was starting over with a clean slate.

The beatings and persecution stopped.

And evangelism began.

chapter twelve

FLYING A KITE

Of all the pastors and prison ministry volunteers who counseled inmates and led Bible studies, Pastor Ruben Viveros was my favorite.

Totally fluent in English and Spanish, Pastor Ruben was all about feeding us the Word of God and keeping our eyes focused on our new lives in Christ. He didn't want us—as new Christians or young Christians—getting hung up on denominational differences like predestination, speaking in tongues, and the role of saints in our lives.

Pastor Ruben kept our noses in pages of Scripture, and I was fine with that. When I got born again, my mind-set was to keep things simple, meaning I thought that being a Christian meant being a Christian. I figured if I kept reading my Bible and learning who God was, then I would be all right. I must have been an eager student because it seemed like Pastor Ruben and I bonded a bit more every time he came to New Folsom, which was every other week, to lead a Bible study in the prison chapel.

One time when our study was over, he motioned me to come over. "Brother Diaz, I have an idea for you."

Pastor Ruben was always calling me "Brother Diaz," a term of endearment. "Sure," I said. "What's up?"

"Over the last few months, I can see that you're influential with the guys. Why don't you start a Bible study in the exercise yard, on your own?"

His suggestion startled me. How could I lead a Bible study? I had no training.

"I don't know if I can teach others," I said. "Don't you have to be qualified?"

Pastor Ruben slapped a hand on my shoulder. "It all starts with your heart," he said. "Why don't you walk out into the yard during your exercise hour and take a picnic table with a couple of the brothers? Sit there and open up the Bible. Read God's Word to each other, which, at the very least, will help your walk in here. And what you're doing will be a witness to other inmates in the yard."

My mind considered what that would look like to others. While many inmates—and all of the prisoners in my unit—knew I was a Christian, some did not. The prison authorities were always changing when we ate and the times we exercised so that we wouldn't interact with the same prisoners all the time. That meant each time I stepped into the New Folsom's exercise yard with a Bible in the crook of my arm, there might be someone who wouldn't admire me for being public about my faith. And prisoners had funny ways of expressing their lack of appreciation, and not all of them were good.

"I think you should do it," Pastor Ruben said, interrupting my thoughts. "You know that I can only come every other week, so that's a long time to go in between Bible studies. I know you're part of some other studies, but starting your own will strengthen your faith and sharpen your understanding of God's Word. Iron sharpens iron, as you know."

I nodded. Pastor Ruben had a point.

"Okay, I'll give it a try," I said.

I asked Abel Ruiz and a couple of other believers in my unit—a guy from MS-13 and a dude from Watts named Anthony—if they were up for it.

They were, especially the guy from MS, who was taking some real punishment inside his unit. He was on the receiving end of hard candy that was even worse than what I had experienced. And yet he didn't back down on his public stance for Christ. That emboldened me.

When we started holding a Bible study in the exercise yard, we took turns reading a verse or two from Scripture and discussing what it meant to us. Quite frankly, I wasn't doing much leading. I acted more as a facilitator, which was perfectly fine with me and with everybody else. Just as important was that everyone in the yard could see what we were doing—four guys sitting on one of the concrete picnic benches with Bibles flipped open to a certain passage. We knew that spoke volumes.

Did anyone come over and ask what we were doing or wonder if they could join us?

Of course not. I should have anticipated that no new prisoners would join our Bible study. To be seen in our company meant you were one of us and likely meant you were dropping out of the gang, which carried serious consequences. But I knew that's what would happen. Inmates weren't open to being evangelized in broad daylight. There was still a code of conduct and certain ways they had to conduct themselves, or they would lose face. Joining a Bible study wasn't part of that.

And then the Lord gave me the idea to pass along a secret note to prisoners who were open to learning more about Him but couldn't be public about their curiosity.

+ + +

Notes that were exchanged among prisoners were known as "kites." Nothing more than a small piece of yellow paper, maybe four inches wide and four inches tall, and filled top to bottom and sometimes both sides with writing in small print, kites were like the notes that junior high kids passed between classes. Kites were usually folded many times until they were the size of a penny, making them easy to pass furtively.

At New Folsom, kites were exchanged among prisoners whenever a shot caller needed to pass a message that someone needed to get hit. Since gang leaders inside New Folsom were used to receiving and passing kites, why not evangelize them by handing them a small note?

I knew that I couldn't walk up to a gang leader in the middle of the exercise yard and offer to shake hands to pass along the note. I couldn't be seen doing that, so I had to be more subtle than that. What I did was put my right arm down by my side and move my hand in such a way that the gang leader would notice that I had a kite wedged between my second and third fingers, meaning I had a message for him. If he was the curious type, he could grab my kite on the sly and keep on walking. No one would be the wiser.

I found the best place to try to pass a kite was when the gang leader and myself were alone, like when we were working the same prison job and no one was paying attention. He would take the kite and slip it into a pants pocket and read it after he returned to his cell.

And that's how an important prison ministry was born.

So what was written in those kites? Believe me, it was nothing profound. I usually wrote something like this:

Hey, I just wanted to reach out to you. I know you can't be seen with me, but that's okay. I just want you to know that if you need prayer, let me know. Just give me a little sign or a nod if you want me to pray for you the next time we see each other, and I'll do it. Remember, God loves you so much. I know you think that God couldn't love you, but He does. John 3:16 says, "For God so loved the world, that he gave his only begotten Son, that whosoever believeth in him should not perish, but have everlasting life." That verse means that anyone who believes in Jesus Christ, God's Son, will be saved. Anyone could be you.

These kites worked instantly. After the exchange of the first kite or two, they would spark conversations between us. Never in the open, of course, but we talked when we could be assured that no one was looking or paying attention to us, like if we were in a chow line or working in the prison laundry room.

Whatever opportunity I found to pass a kite, I took it, but it was always under cover. I never passed the kites out in the open, and neither did my brothers in my Bible study. Instead, we committed ourselves to praying and asking God to move in the hearts of the guys reading our notes.

Most of the time, our kites worked hook, line, and sinker because what we wrote was honest. Here's another kite that I penned:

> I'm pretty sure you know who I am. Every single one of us committed crimes out there. Here's the deal. Christ revealed Himself to me, and I know what He's done in my life. He's changed it big time. I know He can do the same for you. Bottom line, there is no future in what we are doing here. Our homies aren't writing us like they said they would. They aren't taking care of us like they all said they would. We're here. We're stuck. But inside these walls, I've experienced freedom because of what God has done in my life. I'd like to share that with you some time. John 8:32 says, "And ye shall know the truth, and the truth shall make you free." Let me show you how Christ can help you find freedom, even within the walls of this prison.

I was amazed about the impact these kites had. Not only were we receiving head nods from gang leaders asking for prayer, but our Bible studies in the prison chapel became jam-packed. God was touching so many hearts inside that prison—hearts that were tired of living a life of lies, murder, and deceit. We had an incredible number of gang leaders and prisoners come to Christ.

All because we were willing to pass kites.

* * *

I was so encouraged seeing how fast God was moving inside the prison walls. One night I was reading my Bible in my cell when I felt a prompting to pray. I was never taught how to talk to God—I just did it. Here's what I said that night: "Lord, I can see that You're moving through these guys who are coming to these Bible studies. You know they are putting their lives on the line, but I also know it's You doing all the work in here. We're just being used by You. But I was thinking that I want to get a little bit crazier, and here's my idea. If passing along kites works for the inmates, then it has to work for the guards in here. Can you bless this idea of mine?"

So I had this crazy idea of making a kite for our guards. The COs did random counts at night, when they walked from cell to cell, using their flashlights to account for every prisoner. God moved my heart to write a kite for a prison guard that I'd gotten to know a little bit while he was on graveyard shift. Sometimes I would stay up late, praying or reading my Bible, and we'd have a brief interaction.

In mainline, you can put your mail through the wicket in your gate or slide it under your cell door. In this situation, I wrote an evangelistic letter similar to the kites I passed to shot callers. Here's what I wrote:

> I know I'm an inmate, but I also know that you know who I am and what I was. God has set me free, which may sound strange to hear from a prisoner, but it's true. I don't know what your

situation is right now, but I want you to know that I'm praying for you. But more importantly, I'm praying that you, even as a guard, come to Christ. "For God did not send His Son into the world to condemn the world; but that the world through Him might be saved" (John 3:17).

I reached through my wicket and placed the note into a small crevice outside my gate—and waited for the guard to make his rounds. When he came by for the first night head count an hour later, I was half asleep in my bed. I popped out and hit my gate. I didn't say this out loud, but I whispered, "This letter is for you."

The guard grabbed it. A few hours later, I was still half awake the next time he did a head count. This time I remember him stopping at my cell. He didn't say a word, but he looked at me and tapped my gate, which was his way of saying, "Thank you."

That's as close as guards and inmates become in prison. I mean, acknowledging that I wrote him and that he read my words was huge. I felt good knowing that I had witnessed to him and that he made a point to tap my gate, signaling his approval.

◆　◆　◆

I felt God's favor in other areas, including the times I participated in mandated, court-ordered programs that prisoners had to go to during their prison stay. They were called Victim Awareness meetings.

Every Tuesday morning, I was among eight prisoners who met with our counselor, a black gentleman named Mr. White. He was down-to-earth and not stern—a nice-guy demeanor that he used to get us to talk about crimes. His job was to get us to share what we were learning through this process of incarceration, what we've learned about our crimes, what we've learned about our victims, and how we feel about our crimes now. His big question was summed up like this: *If you had a second chance, would you do it differently, or would it be the same result?*

The group setting was kept small to promote transparency, but that only went so far. Even though we all knew each other, none of us felt safe to say what we were really thinking. If you think about it, we were all predators in there, when it gets to the nitty gritty. And yet, for some reason, it felt good sharing my experiences because I could talk about how I had changed in prison because of my relationship with Christ.

One time Mr. White started the proceedings by saying, "I know there is a code of conduct in here: you don't snitch, you don't rat on anybody. But think about how far that has gotten you. Take Diaz as an example here. They gave him extra years just because he didn't want to tell on his homies. His homies are out there or maybe they are locked up, but why would you take the blame all by yourself because of a street code?

"Now he's sitting here with us in this group, and he took the whole case on himself. But beyond that, we all know this guy has risked his life in here by becoming a Christian. Look at the changes he has made. I looked at his file, and this is a guy who has been in the system since he was eleven years old. Every year since then, there was not one year where he was not incarcerated for at least a short time. Maybe it was three months, six months, or nine months, but there has never been one year since the age of eleven where he had not done time.

"So what does that say to us as a society? It's telling us that it's his life. It's telling us that he's most comfortable inside walls. How do you feel about that?"

That's known as teeing it up.

I followed Mr. White's lead and talked about how my crimes and unlawful behavior impacted victims. I shared openly, and there was never a time when I was ashamed or embarrassed.

"You know me. I've been to the SHU. We all have different stories, but a crime is still a crime. I think about every robbery I've done. I can picture the fear in those families when we came into their homes and tied them up. I can see their faces. I look at myself now, as a Christian, and I truly understand that I deserve to be in here. Society is much safer with me in prison."

Not too many guys said those types of things. If there was one thing I learned in prison, it was this: No one was guilty. No one ever told you to your face that they did it. Their reluctance to take ownership of their deeds reminded me of the time I had been arrested late one night and driven to the Glass House—the Parker Center Police Station in downtown LA. The Glass House served as a substation before the prisoners were transferred to Men's Central Jail.

I was tossed into a holding cell containing a half dozen people who'd just been arrested on the street. One guy—a grown man—was bawling. I mean, he was really crying his head off. This was in the middle of the night, and he was carrying on like there was no tomorrow. "I didn't do it! I didn't do it!" he cried out. "They got the wrong man!"

He not only had the attention of the guards, but he had our attention. We wanted him to shut up, or we would wring this guy's neck.

One of the deputy sheriffs dropped by to see what all the commotion was about. He was one of those good old boys who'd been around the block in his police cruiser a few times.

"Yeah, nobody in here has done anything," he said with heavy sarcasm. "We're still looking for the guys that did y'all's crimes. As soon as we find the guys who done it, you're all going home."

I may have felt like that crying fool one time and never admitted to anything, but when Christ touched my heart, I knew I had to take full responsibility for my actions. I was a sinner. I did those horrible things. I needed to pay my debt to society because of my crimes. I was okay with that. I was okay that they had shut the door on me. I belonged there because of the crimes I had done.

✦ ✦ ✦

One Tuesday, just before another Victim Awareness meeting, I remember running across Matthew 5:26, in which Jesus said during the Sermon on the Mount that in a dispute with an adversary, you may get thrown into prison and you will not get out until you have paid every last penny.

I thought of that when it became my turn to speak. Under Mr. White's prompting to share our feelings, I said this: "What I have done in the past is without dispute. I committed crimes, many of them. I terrorized the streets of Los Angeles. I terrorized families and victims. There are victims left and right from the terror I caused. Because of what I did, there is no better place for me than in prison. I deserve every bit of this."

"Thank you, Mr. Diaz," Mr. White said.

What I left unsaid was my understanding that I deserved everything I had coming to me, but Christ forgave me for my horrible sins and changed my life. That didn't change the debt I owed society or make things any better with the victims or their families, but I still felt like I was on the right track and was okay with being killed in prison or whatever was going to happen with me.

I saw so many prisoners who attempted to justify their crimes. They lied to the counselors, lied to the psychiatrists, and lied to their fellow inmates. The way I saw things, until you admitted that you were the predator, you were stuck emotionally and psychologically.

I started noticing that the counselors were referring to me as an example of someone who had changed and whose change was genuine. They had seen a lot of "jailhouse religion" over the years—prisoners who experience dramatic turnarounds as the result of a spiritual conversion. They had witnessed prisoners up for parole "faking the funk" and pretending to be Christians to score brownie points with the parole board.

And yet, these counselors and prison psychologists spoke respect-fully, if not glowingly, about how I had changed since coming out of the SHU. While that was nice to hear, I kept my head down. This was a time to stay humble.

That was because I had done the crime, which meant I had to do the time.

chapter thirteen

LETTERS FROM FRANCES

Not long after I was moved from the SHU to mainline, I noticed a letter placed in my wicket.

That was unusual. The only person writing me was my mother, and her letters were becoming more and more infrequent as the years behind bars passed by.

I opened the letter. The cursive handwriting on beige stationery was beautiful:

Dear Darwin:

I hope you're doing well. During my last visit, the guards told me that you had been transferred out of solitary confinement. I thank God for that.

I hope you remember me coming by your cell. God has laid it on my heart to pray for you and tell you that God has great plans for you. Proverbs 3:5–6 says, "Trust in the Lord with all thine heart; and lean not unto thine own understanding. In all thy ways acknowledge him, and he shall direct thy paths."

May God bless you and protect you.

Sincerely,

Frances Proctor

So that was her name—Frances Proctor. I imagined what she looked like since I could see only her bony legs while I was in the SHU. From her voice, I believed she was a kind and soft-spoken middle-aged black woman, probably in her late fifties or early sixties. I imagined that she had flecks of gray on her shoulder-length hair and black-framed glasses perched on her nose.

I immediately wrote her back and shared the exciting news that I had given my heart to Christ. I didn't tell her in full detail what happened—I'm referring to the movie-like "screening" of my life and Jesus' crucifixion on the concrete wall—but I did write that Christ met me in my cell in a miraculous way and that I saw a prison chaplain who explained the gospel to me afterward. I also described how I got on my knees in my cell and prayed for God to forgive me for all the crimes I had committed.

I didn't have to wait long to receive a reply from Frances. She described the sheer joy she felt and rejoiced that a "lost sheep" had been found. Then she shared Luke 15 where Jesus said, "I say unto you, that likewise joy shall be in heaven over one sinner that repenteth, more than over ninety and nine just persons, which need no repentance" (Luke 15:7 KJV).

We continued to exchange letters until a couple of months later when a guard passed by with an announcement. "The LA group is here for their monthly Bible study. If you want to go, step forward on your gate," he said.

I didn't know about this Bible study, which was likely sponsored by a prison ministry visiting New Folsom. No matter. I was up for a Bible study any time. So was my good buddy Abel Ruiz.

The guard unlocked my gate and directed a half dozen

prisoners—all black except for Abel and me—to a break room along a hallway. As we approached, I heard voices inside. One of them sounded very familiar. In fact, I knew it was the black woman who visited me in the SHU.

I stepped into the break room and saw her sitting at a table with three African American men dressed in suits. She was wearing a print dress and looked just as I had pictured her—an older black woman with a radiant countenance.

"Frances Proctor?" I asked.

The older woman rose to her feet.

"Dah-win?" She looked as stunned as I was.

"Yes, it's me."

Then she exploded in praise to God. "Hallelujah! Look at this! Look at what God has done!"

Then she approached and grabbed my right arm. Turning to the African American men in the room, she said, "This is Dah-win. This is the one I was telling you about in solitary."

One of the deacons said, "Yes, I remember you describing this young man to us. Look at him! This is amazing!"

Broad smiles burst out, and Frances held out her arms. She wanted a hug, and I gave her one while a guard—normally as serious as a funeral director—watched with a thin smile creased across his lips.

After our Bible study, Frances wrote me more often. She would share what her six boys were doing—four were pastors and two were studying to enter the ministry. She said she was a single-parent mom who worked at the *Los Angeles Times* as an administrative assistant. She lived in South-Central LA and attended Triedstone Missionary Baptist Church on West Adams in the Lakewood area of downtown LA.

I was astounded to hear that she and her fellow church members rode a bus from Los Angeles to New Folsom on the last Thursday of every month to conduct prison ministry. Because the trip was so long, they stayed overnight in the Sacramento area before returning to Southern California.

All I can say about my spiritual mentor is what a truly amazing person she was. If you've seen the 2015 movie *War Room* and recall Miss Clara, the elderly black woman who was a prayer warrior, then you have a pretty good picture of who Frances Proctor was.

A saint.

+ + +

I don't know why, but the prison authorities never gave me a cellmate during my first year in mainline. Mind you, I wasn't complaining because you never knew who you'd get, even though you could figure that your "bunkie" had been convicted of murder, usually in the first degree. In other words, you weren't going to get St. Francis of Assisi assigned to the bunk above you at New Folsom.

Another reason I liked being by myself—besides having uninterrupted time to read my Bible—was because I was a very neat person. I liked to keep a spick-and-span cell that was clean enough to, well, eat off the floor.

My cell floor was spotless because I waxed my concrete floor. I mean, I *really* waxed my floor. I waxed my concrete floor until I could practically see my reflection.

It all started when I requested a gallon of industrial floor wax from the commissary. I poured a healthy amount onto the floor—about the size of a hubcap—and got on my knees. Then I took a shower towel and slowly, from left to right, used a windshield-wiper motion to spread the wax, being careful not to rub the cleaning solution into the concrete but glide my towel evenly from left to right.

I worked my way from the front of my cell toward the back, like painting myself into a corner. When I finished my last gliding motion, I hopped on the toilet, reached down and finished the last section of floor, and then jumped to my bunk, where I hung out until the wax dried to a shiny finish, just as if I had used a buffer.

Word got around that Casey Diaz had the shiniest cell floor in New Folsom. My counselor, Mr. White, heard the commotion and visited one day.

"Wow, man, that's like the military," he said. "This floor looks nice. You did this yourself?"

"Yes, sir. I sure did." It felt good to get noticed for doing something positive.

"Would you like a job waxing floors around here?"

And get out of my cell and earn a few dollars?

"Sure," I replied. "That would be great."

The next thing I knew, Mr. White recommended that I get a prison job waxing the floors and hallways in my unit.

The guards gave me a yellow janitorial bucket on rollers and a mop. I filled the bucket with two gallons of wax but took the mop off the end of the broomstick and replaced it with a shower towel, which I dipped into the wax solution. And then I worked my right arm from left to right, left to right, spreading the wax on the floor as evenly as I could. The prison had a buffer machine, and boy, did that make polishing the wax easy!

I did such a good job that I was asked to wax the floors in the administrative offices, hallways, and chapel. It wasn't long before the guards had me going everywhere, so much so that my days speeded up tremendously. After being "slammed down" in solitary, locked away in that cell for twenty-three hours a day, being outside my cell for six to eight hours a day was a revelation. I loved working, burning off some energy, and feeling useful.

I needed that because when I was alone in my cell, it was getting harder to do time. The walls had a way of reminding me that I wasn't free. In fact, when I spoke to other inmates about this phenomenon, we all felt that the walls talked to us in a certain way. I know people on the outside won't understand this, but when you're locked up inside a six-by-eight cell—with less than fifty square feet of living space—those walls have a way of getting in your head.

After two years in California Youth Authority, three years in the SHU, and more than a year and a half in mainline, the thought of serving my entire sentence of twelve years, eight months seemed way off in the future. Being locked up was getting to me. I still had more than five years to go, which was really depressing.

The prison counselors must have spotted how down I was because I was told to take an antidepressant called Sinequan. I had been pre-scribed Sinequan (also known as Doxepin) back in the SHU, and I didn't like the side effects—dizziness, nausea, and bouts of vomiting.

This time around, I decided to do something about it. When a prison nurse dropped by my gate with a capsule of Sinequan, I popped the medication into my mouth and took a swig of water—but I didn't swallow the pill.

"Let me see," she said.

I opened my mouth wide and stuck out my tongue. She leaned forward and peered inside. "You're good," she said, moving on to the next cell.

I had successfully hidden the capsule between my back molars and my gums. When the nurse left, I flushed the antidepressant down the toilet. In the future, I would never get caught not taking my medication.

Even though my attitude brightened from having fooled the nurse, that didn't sweep away the feelings of depression.

Once again it was the walls, which had a unique way of remind-ing me that I was still an inmate, still locked up, and that I was going to be there for a long time. The soundtrack of my life would continue to be the sounds of cell doors locking, buzzers ringing, and guards barking orders.

Then there were the times when I'd be sitting on my bunk bed, listening to other prisoners talking and laughing with other inmates from their cells. Since I was an outcast, I almost felt like they were having fun and I wasn't, which got me feeling the blues again.

◆　◆　◆

What got me down the most was calling my mom. She couldn't call me, so I had to call her. Back in those days, that meant a collect call, meaning the receiving party agreed to pay the outrageous long-distance charges AT&T charged in those days. Because collect calls were so expensive—several bucks a minute—I only called Mom once a month and limited the call to five minutes.

Hearing her voice for a few minutes got me depressed when I thought about all that she had done for me. She had left El Salvador for a better life in America, for a better opportunity for me—but I squandered her efforts and her courage by falling in with a gang and participating in all sorts of heinous crimes. The feelings of regret that filled my heart were difficult to shake off.

You blew it, man. Now you're locked up and can't do anything. You've been locked up since you were sixteen, and you're not getting out of here for at least four or five more years.

That's when another wave of depression would come all over me again.

One time I closed my eyes and imagined what it would be like to walk out of New Folsom and sit under the shade of an oak tree. How cool would that be? A simple act like leaning my back against a tree trunk and breathing in freedom seemed like heaven to me. Those thoughts momentarily lifted the fog of depression, as did reminding myself that the beatings had stopped. That was huge, and I knew I should be thankful to the Lord for His protection.

I was thankful . . . until the next time I felt like the walls were closing in on me.

✦ ✦ ✦

After a year in mainline, I got my first bunkie.

His name was Benson. Well, I never learned his first name. I called him Benson, and he called me Diaz. He was a tall, lanky white guy, probably six feet, four inches, who was a couple of years older than me.

In the movies, when a new cellmate enters the picture, they show the two prisoners getting along like peas in a pod, sharing every detail of the felonies they committed. *Partners in crime.*

The reality is far different. Prisoners, upon meeting each other, will share what they were convicted for, but they rarely disclose the details. That's information that can be used against you—not in a court of law but in the court of prison life.

Benson and I got the preliminaries out in the open right away. He told me he was behind bars for first-degree murder, and I said I had a second-degree murder rap plus multiple felonies for robbery. On that scorecard, we were roughly even.

He wasn't a Christian, but he didn't make fun of me for reading the Bible. He smoked, which I found disgusting. It might be hard to believe in this day and age, but back then, inmates were given cigarettes and matches along with prison blues and toiletries. I didn't smoke, but Benson puffed on cigarettes all day long.

I wouldn't say that Benson and I became friends. I was okay with him, and he was okay with me. We gave each other space.

Benson was in the eleventh year of a long sentence—I can't remember the length. He was twenty-five years old, three years older than me. Shortly after he started sharing a cell with me, he was up for parole. Once prisoners become eligible for release, they can request a hearing each year, although nine times out of ten it's a fruitless exercise. The situation is much different today, but back then, parole boards didn't release you until you served every last day of your sentence.

Since he was nearing the end of his prison term, Benson thought he had a shot. I wished him good luck as he was escorted from his cell to the parole hearing. A couple of hours later, before lunch chow, Benson returned to our cell and didn't look good at all. He appeared to be shaken, distraught. Maybe he got a firm no and a lecture about how he would serve every single day of his sentence. Maybe the parole board *added* time to his prison term.

"You don't look so hot. What happened?" I asked. "Did they say no?"

"No, not yet. They're still deliberating."

And then the strangest thing happened—Benson started crying. I'd never seen him shed a tear about anything, but he had the waterworks going now.

I leaned in and whispered, "Hey, man, don't do that. If someone walks by and sees you crying, you're going to get yourself killed in here."

Do prisoners get killed for crying in prison? If you're perceived as showing weakness, the answer is definitely yes. If you show vulnerability, you're done.

"You don't understand. Going through everything this morning got to me, man. I don't think my sister and mom will ever forgive me."

"Dude, it's your mother and sister. I'm pretty sure they will forgive you for whatever you did. It can't be that bad."

"No, no. You don't understand. They will never forgive me. Never."

Benson handed me a manila file folder from his hearing. "Here. Read this."

The file contained his paperwork as well as a synopsis of the crime he committed. Apparently, when Benson was fourteen years old, he was afraid of his father, who regularly beat the snot out of him.

One day his parents left on a business trip. Benson was left behind. Their home was out in the country, and the nearest neighbor was a mile away.

Benson was home alone when his father returned. He had apparently forgotten something and left Benson's mom at a restaurant while he drove back to the house.

Nasty words were exchanged between Benson and his father, and tension escalated. When his father walked to another part of the house, Benson went to the garage, where a gun safe was located. Benson knew where the key was located, so he opened up the lockbox and pulled out a .38 revolver, which he loaded. Then he wetted down a towel.

Benson snuck up on his father and shot him twice in the back of the head, killing him. The wet towel around the revolver supposedly dampened the sound of shots being fired, but the nearest neighbor was so far away that it really didn't matter. Benson wrapped his father's body in a living room curtain, dropped the dead body in the trunk of his car, and buried his father in a makeshift grave out in the woods.

When Benson's father didn't return for his mother who was waiting in a restaurant, police were called. An open-and-shut case sent Benson to California Youth Authority, followed by a transfer to an adult prison when he turned eighteen.

After I closed the folder, I didn't say anything. Benson was right—his mother and sister would likely never forgive him.

That afternoon, Benson was granted parole. How or why that happened was beyond me. Maybe it was because Benson was a smart guy. He'd gotten his high school diploma and AA degree while in prison and was a TA—teacher's assistant—in other classes for prisoners. For some reason, the University of California at San Diego (UCSD) had given him a grant covering tuition, an apartment, and food money so he could attend college there. He didn't have to pay for a thing because he qualified for a state program that helped inmates adjust to freedom. Everything was paid for at UCSD.

After Benson came back with the good news, I watched him pack up and walk out of our cell for the last time. Witnessing his walk to freedom depressed me. I was angry, too, but my faith was solid. I knew God was in control. I had to deal with my emotions and not let them get the best of me.

A few months later, I was in my cell, doing my thing when I heard commotion outside my gate. I looked up—and there was Benson!

He wasn't dressed in prison blues but in civilian clothes. He looked genuinely happy to see me.

"Hey, Diaz!"

"Benson! What the heck are you doing here, man?"

"I'm here to talk to some prisoners about being on the outside. You know, what it's like out there."

"You doin' good?"

"Real good. I'm going to school at UCSD. I've adjusted pretty well, man. I got a job, and I'm keeping my nose clean."

Benson looked past me and took in the surroundings. "Looks like the same cell," he said, stating the obvious.

"Yeah, man. You're looking at the penthouse suite." I laid on the sarcasm fairly thick.

"At least the floor is still shiny."

I chuckled. "You haven't forgotten. Hey, how's the food out there?"

"It's good. It's amazing how quickly good food becomes normal again."

We made small talk for a few more minutes, and then I watched him turn and go.

Now I get to see this guy walk away twice, I thought. *And I'm still stuck here.*

I still had five years to go.

I prayed that the time would go fast.

chapter fourteen

CHANGES AHEAD

I didn't get a new cell mate after Benson got paroled.

I was fine with that since I had grown used to being by myself after three years of solitary. I liked my quiet time with the Lord. I liked my routine. It's how I did time. I didn't want to make waves.

I'm not saying that I didn't want to be around others. I knew it was going to be a good day when I had a Bible study or chapel service to attend because I could interact with my brothers in Christ. I craved Christian fellowship, and studying God's Word with other believers as well as curious seekers filled my emotional sails.

My best friend at New Folsom was Abel Ruiz. He was in the cell opposite mine, so even if we were locked up we could look at each other and chat like we were in a coffeehouse. He was my road dog—someone you hung out with in the chow hall and exercise yard, someone you did life with inside state prison. Abel let me use his Walkman audio-cassette player. He shared Bible commentaries with me. If I ran out of toothpaste, he had an extra tube. He looked out for me, and I did the same for him.

There were times when one of us would be "hard-timing," meaning one of us was down about being locked up for so long. Abel had a wife and kids on the outside, so it was understandable that his low moments were lower than mine. He'd often tell me how grieved he was to miss out on so much—and he was right. His heart ached for his family. I did my best to pick him up and be a good listener.

Abel was a good dude. When I was hard-timing, I talked to him about things I couldn't share with anyone else—like how I felt the walls were closing in or whether someone would *still* try to take me out.

We were sitting in the exercise yard one day, back when I was still receiving hard candy every now and then. I told Abel that I was having a hard day and thinking about hurting and maiming a particular inmate who seemed to have it out for me. (This happened after I took things out on Spanky and pummeled him in my cell.)

Abel listened to me vent, and when I was done, he said, "You gotta calm down, man. Just let it be. Come on, take an extra breath. Remember, you got away with it once. You can't make another mistake in here. You don't want to give the warden any reason to add time to your sentence."

Abel was right. I had to act wisely. I had to see the big picture, which was doing time without drawing attention to myself. In other words, laying low.

Then came the day when Abel returned from a parole hearing with the hugest grin on his face. He had been released! While I was genuinely happy for him, the news still felt like a sucker punch to the gut. My road dog was leaving me . . . the guy who I trusted with my life and who'd been incredibly helpful to me in my young faith. Abel and I had grown close, but now he was packing up.

When it came time to say our final goodbyes, he dropped by my gate. "You're going to be all right," he said. "I'll make sure I write you and send you a package every now and then."

"You don't have to do that, man. Really, I'm going to be fine."

I wanted to give Abel an out. One thing I'd learned after nearly a decade behind bars was that ten times out of ten, ex-cons *don't* write when they get out. It was nothing personal; that's just the way things were. (In fact, Abel would write only once and that was it.)

Abel reached over to his left wrist and unfastened a cheap watch that he was allowed to wear in prison. He bent over and slid the plastic timepiece under my gate. "Keep it," he said.

"No, man, you don't have to do that."

"It's okay, Casey."

I put on the watch and beamed. Then I wished Abel all the best.

Five minutes later, I looked through my window, which overlooked the yard. The rectangular window was five inches wide and probably two feet tall. From my perch, I watched Abel walk away.

Abel was a free man, but I still had more than four years to go.

I continued to polish floors and either participated in or led three or four Bible studies during the week, which drew twenty-five to thirty-five men. Prisoners were coming to Christ, and you could say that there was a mini-revival at New Folsom. Our Sunday morning chapel services, led by the prison chaplain or an out-of-town pastor, were drawing between 150 and 200 men.

After two years in mainline, and with around four and a half years left on my sentence, I was up for parole. Whenever I attended my annual parole hearings, I never held out any hopes of an early release.

✦　✦　✦

A guard escorted me to a bench outside a small room where the parole board met.

I took a seat and waited my turn. Then I heard footsteps coming my way. Another correctional officer was escorting a man in a dark business suit into the foyer. I recognized him. He was Pastor Charles, a Los Angeles pastor who came up to New Folsom every few weeks to lead a Bible study in prison.

I gave Pastor Charles a glance that said, *What are you doing here?* He couldn't be coming on my behalf because I wasn't going anywhere.

Pastor Charles recognized the look. He took a seat next to me and patted my knee.

"I'm here for you," he said.

"What are you talking about?"

"I heard you're up for parole today. I just want to pray for you before you go in there."

"That's nice of you, but it's awkward all the same."

"Awkward? What do you mean?"

"This is my yearly parole hearing. They have to give me one, although they aren't going to release me. It's not like I'm going anywhere."

"Well, I just wanted to pray for you."

I wasn't about to pass on prayer, so I lowered my head and listened to Pastor Charles pray out loud: "God, have mercy on Darwin. If it's for him to stay, we're okay with that, Lord. You're the author of our lives, of every minute of every day. May Your will be done with the parole board today."

I didn't have to wait long until I was called in. Pastor Charles asked a guard if he could accompany me, and he was given permission to do so. When we walked through the door into a small room, we sat down together and faced the parole board.

Three men and two women—a five-person panel—held my fate in their hands. The makeup of the parole board often changes, but I recognized the no-nonsense chairperson who sat in the middle of the dais—Maximum John.

At least that's what we called him in mainline. Every prisoner knew that if Maximum John showed up at your parole hearing, you weren't going anywhere. You might as well say goodbye and return to your cell. Every inmate knew how tough he was. He was the type of guy who'd keep a model prisoner inside the prison walls until his very last week. If he could hold you another day, he would. That's how tremendously harsh he was.

Maximum John was a heavyset older man with a full white beard. All he needed was a woolen stocking cap and he would look like Santa Claus. But there was no "Ho, ho, ho" or holiday cheer in his demeanor. With reading glasses perched at the end of his nose, he had a way of looking at you in an intimidating fashion. Whenever he looked up from his notes, he looked at you with his eyes, not through the eyeglasses.

Maximum John opened up my file and reviewed his notes.

"I see you've finished all your court-ordered classes," he said, which was true. He was referring to the Victim Awareness classes.

"Yes, sir," I replied.

Maximum John paused, then looked at me past the eyeglasses resting precariously on the tip of nose. "Why do you think you're fit for parole?" he asked.

I anticipated this question. Most prisoners, upon hearing that query, would talk about how they've taken every Victim Awareness class possible and earned three college degrees, volunteered to help the mentally challenged in prison, and gotten high marks for kitchen duty. In other words, they would paint themselves in the best possible light because no one wants to stay an extra day in prison.

I don't know what possessed me, but that morning I told Maximum John and the parole board, "I'm not fit for parole. I understand what I'm guilty of. I have a debt that I owe society and the streets of Los Angeles for victimizing them. Because of what I did, I understand that I need to pay the very last day in here, so to answer your question, I'm not fit for parole. I deserve to stay in here. Sure, I've learned a great deal since I arrived at New Folsom. I've completed the mandatory courses that the court has ordered me to take. But I'm okay with staying as long as you want to keep me here. I'm not trying to look for an early parole date or anything. I'm fine with where things are."

The parole board wasn't used to hearing a prisoner speak like that. An interesting thing happened—all pretenses were swept away. I had been real with my feelings, which prompted a series of questions from the parole board members. They asked me about my life growing up, why I joined Rockwood, about my crimes, and what I thought about gangs now.

And then the questions stopped. I was dismissed and told to wait outside while the panel deliberated my fate.

◆　◆　◆

Pastor Charles followed me to the foyer. "What do you think?" he asked.

"What do I think about what?"

"So how do you think you did?"

"Look. What do you want me to say? I'm cool. Maximum John's in there, so I'm not getting my hopes up. They're going to deny me parole and that's that."

"So you don't think you're going home?"

"Are you kidding? Don't forget, I'm in here for some serious charges. It's not like I stole a candy bar. I'm guilty as guilty can be, and there was stuff I didn't get caught for. Apart from that, they can do anything they want, and I'm quite fine with that."

Fifteen, twenty minutes passed by. Pastor Charles and I made small talk about what books in the Bible I was reading. Then we were called back in.

While we were finding our seats and getting settled, Maximum John called out to Pastor Charles, "Are there any good places to eat where you live?"

Now, that seemed like a strange question, especially because my pastor friend lived in South-Central LA, where he was a pastor of an Assemblies of God church. He was an educated Christian man who'd graduated from USC.

"There are a whole lot of good places to eat where I live," he said.

What was this all about?

One of the panel members directed a similar question to me. "Mr. Diaz, where you going to eat today?"

Now I was really confused. These were crazy questions. Maybe they were referring to lunch. "Well, I know chow is about to happen, so I'd really like to get out of here so I can get a hot plate," I said. "Otherwise, I'm eating a bologna sandwich, so a hot plate would be good."

Several of the board members gave each other knowing looks, including Maximum John, who looked as jolly as a Santa at a mall department store.

"Mr. Diaz," he said, "we don't let anyone out early, especially on serious charges such as yours, but we believe that something special has really taken place in your life. We also believe that you became a changed young man in here. The very fact that you've turned your back on your gang members speaks volumes. We know all about the beatings you took for doing that. There's documentation and proof in your file. You've apparently gone through some extreme changes inside this prison and risked your life for what you believe. You're to be commended for taking those actions."

"Thank you," I managed.

"We know jailhouse religion when we see it," Maximum John continued. "We don't think this is it. We believe something unique has happened in your life, so therefore, this parole board, with the power invested in it by the California Department of Corrections and Rehabilitation, have decided to grant you parole. Immediately."

I lost it. I completely lost it. *I was being released?* That's when everything went into slow motion for me. Some paperwork was pushed in front of me to sign. I have no idea what I gave my autograph to, but I couldn't believe they were letting me out nearly five years early!

I couldn't turn on my heels and walk out of there, however. As I expected, there was a process to follow, which meant I wouldn't be freed until I spent one more night in lock-up.

◆   ◆   ◆

The following morning, I packed my belongings. It didn't take long to throw what few clothes I had, some toiletries, my Bible, and a couple of Spanish-language Bibles someone had given me into a cardboard box. I did not call my mother to let her know that I had been paroled and was coming home early. One part of me wanted to surprise her, but I also didn't want to give her something more to worry about.

When two guards arrived after morning chow, I was ready to go. I looked around at my cell and my gate one last time. This was it; I was really leaving this prison chamber behind. It felt real because I wasn't handcuffed or constrained in any way.

I was led to a room where I was fingerprinted and then ordered to take off all my clothes. I stood buck naked in front of a cameraman who snapped shots of me from every angle. The purpose was to see if I had received any new tattoos while I was at New Folsom—tattoos that would reveal sympathies to gangs or certain factions.

Then I was given a California ID card since I needed government-issued identification to do just about anything on the outside—get a job, get a driver's license, get a bank account, get an apartment . . . the list was long. Then I was handed two hundred dollars in "gate money"—cash to pay for a bus or train ticket back to Los Angeles. Once I was out the back door of New Folsom, I would be driven to a nearby transportation depot and dropped off. What I did next was entirely up to me.

After all the pictures were taken, I was led through several more doors and checkpoints until I reached the last door—a glass door like you'd see in any office building. When I stepped out into the sunshine—and breathed in the air of freedom—I couldn't believe this was happening. Then, as I walked out, I spotted two white men in dark business suits and sunglasses standing next to a beige government-issue van. They looked like they were from the FBI. One of the agents perked up. He took two steps toward me.

"Darwin Diaz?"

I was surprised he wanted to speak to me. "Yeah?"

"Please turn around and put your hands behind your back."

My stomach dropped. I didn't know what this was about. Could it be another case that I had long forgotten about and now I had to do the time for that crime in a *federal* prison? I didn't know.

A thousand things were flying through my mind at that moment. The agent handcuffed me and put chains around my waist. Now I was under full-restraint. Again. He walked me over to the van and assisted me onto a bench row inside the van.

Before the agent closed the door, I asked him, "What's going on? Who are you guys?"

"We're with the INS."

The Immigration and Naturalization Service.

This federal agency in the Department of Justice enforced laws and regulations regarding the admission of foreign-born persons to the United States.

Sure, I was born in El Salvador, but I had my green card. I was legally inside the United States.

"Do you have any family in El Salvador?" he asked.

"No, I don't. All my family is here."

"We're going to process you at the federal detention center, and then we'll take it from there. We'll give you information as we go."

And then the van door slammed shut.

✦   ✦   ✦

I suppose I should have been excited about being outdoors and seeing tree-lined boulevards and busy strip malls as we drove along the thoroughfare. There were people walking into restaurants and shops and kids playing in front yards—scenes I hadn't witnessed in a dozen years. Instead, I was lost in thought, wondering what it was that I had done to incur the attention of the INS.

Would the INS really send me back to El Salvador? The possibility seemed inconceivable. El Salvador was a foreign country to me. I didn't know anyone there. I no longer had any family there. Not only did I know next to nothing about this Central American country, my Spanish sucked.

For some reason, though, I wasn't worried. I knew God hadn't abandoned me after I left my prison cell. Besides, what did I have to complain about? At least I was out. At least I'd wind up a free man—in this country or in El Salvador. And if I would be put on a plane to El Salvador, then God had His reasons for sending me to Central America. I took the attitude that I was along for the ride— and God had His hands on the steering wheel.

At the detention center, the INS agent I had been interacting with the most—I'll call him Agent Turner—informed me that because I was a felon who had committed a serious crime and wasn't born here, I was eligible to be deported to El Salvador, the country of my birth.

"But I have a green card," I said, referring to the permit that allows foreign nationals to live and work permanently in the United States. "You can't deport me if I'm here legally."

"We can for aggravated felonies," the INS agent replied.

My heart sank. A second-degree murder rap was a felony. How "aggravated" it was, I didn't know, but things sure weren't looking good.

Agent Turner unshackled me and led me to a metal holding tank, where I met two guys from Mexico. A rotary phone hung on the wall with instructions in English and Spanish on how to make collect calls. I wondered if I should phone my mother and explain the pickle I was in. But there was nothing she could do. Calling her would only add a mountain of stress to her life.

"*¿A dónde vas?*" asked one of the other guys in the holding tank. I'll call him Miguel. *Where are you going?*

Like I said, my Spanish was rudimentary at best. "It looks like El Salvador," I replied in English.

"You have family down there?" Miguel replied in English that was better than my Spanish.

"Nope. I don't have anybody down there."

"Wow, man. You mean your folks are out here?"

"Yeah, I have my mom," I said. "I still have my dad, but we don't get along very well."

With the ice broken, the three of us conversed in English, which was surprisingly good. I explained how I had been paroled only to be bound and shackled by INS agents and being told I would be deported to a country that I didn't know except from stories my parents told me.

"But you know what?" I said. "I'm not worried about what's going to happen to me."

Miguel and his compadre, whom I'll call Luis, looked baffled.

"How come?" Miguel asked.

"Because God did something to me while I was in prison, and I became a Christian. That happened a couple of years ago, while I was in there. I'm not worried about what's going to happen in my life. I know wherever He takes me, I'll have peace because I'm secure in Him."

Miguel, who was clearly more interested in my story than Luis, didn't believe me. "Are you sure you're going to be okay?"

"Yeah, I am. What are you? A Catholic?"

"Yeah, I'm Catholic. But I don't practice or anything."

"You have a family?"

"Yeah, a wife and kids. I'm worried about what's going to happen to them."

I recalled the Bible studies in which we were taught to share our faith. A few verses from the "Roman Road" came to mind. I explained how we have all sinned and come short of the glory of God (Romans 3:23) and how the wages of sin is death but God wants to give us the gift of eternal life with Him if we will only believe in His Son, Jesus Christ (Romans 6:23).

"Everyone who calls on the name of the Lord will be saved," I said. "That's what the Bible teaches us in Romans 10:13. Listen, we are all in need of a Savior. Think about what God can do in your life when you completely surrender to Him and repent. When you do that and give your life to Christ, God will change everything. He can use you."

I was on a roll. "By the grace of God, I'm able to talk to you today, in this holding cell. I could have lost my life in there, but God spared me. God can spare your life, too, but you need to turn to Christ. Tomorrow isn't promised to anybody. You could lose your life en route to wherever you're going. You're going to Mexico soon. And then what?"

I saw that Miguel was thinking. Maybe he was involved in the drug cartels, where life was cheap. Maybe he witnessed shootings and decapitations and knew he could be next.

"Listen, hell is a very real thing. And eternity is a really long time. Would you like to give your life to Christ and know that when you die you will be with Jesus, in heaven?"

Miguel didn't hesitate. "I want to give my life to Christ," he said.

Right there in the holding cell, I asked him to bow his head, close his eyes, and repeat the sinner's prayer after me. When we were done, I gave him a hug. Then I suddenly remembered that I had two Spanish Bibles, still in their original plastic wrapping, in my cardboard box.

I hopped up and walked over to the bars just as Agent Turner was walking by.

"Sir, can you do me a favor? Can you go over to my box and get me one of the Spanish Bibles?"

Agent Turner ran a hand through his hair. "Sure," he said.

When I received the Spanish Bible, I unwrapped the clear plastic and encouraged Miguel to start reading the gospel of John as well as Psalms and Proverbs.

"You just surrendered your heart to Christ, and now it's your responsibility to be different, to act differently. We don't know how all this is going to work out, but I do know that God's going to do something with your life because you belong to Him. You have to hope and trust in God throughout this time. Look, we put so much time into trusting other human beings that have failed us. Here we are trusting God, whom we have never seen, but we know He's true. Something's happening in your heart. Even right now. You know that. When you place your trust in Him, you'll find that your entire life will change."

Miguel was in tears. I came alongside him on the bench and wrapped an arm around his shoulder. I couldn't help but notice that Luis was paying close attention to what was going on, so I turned to him.

"Listen, don't leave this building, don't leave this place, without giving your heart to Christ too," I said to Luis. Then I shared my testimony about leaving my gang and my shot-caller status. When he heard that, he understood that I wasn't just some random gang member trying to play the religious card. I was somebody who was being real about what my life was like before I surrendered to Christ.

"How about you, man? What's stopping you from coming to God?" I asked. "What are you afraid of?"

"Well, I have a wife and kids too. I'm worried what's going to happen to them when I get deported."

"Well, this is really happening. You're going back to Mexico. I'm going back to El Salvador. Thank God, I'm not married or have children, but you are, so you have a responsibility to them. You need God by your side. That's the only way you're going to get through this."

The next thing I knew, I was standing in a circle and holding hands with Luis and Miguel and leading Luis to Christ. When we were done, I approached the holding cell bars. Agent Turner was in the vicinity again.

"Hey, I hate to bother you a second time, but there's a second Bible in Spanish in my box. Can you get that one for me, please?"

"No problem," the INS agent replied.

I handed the Bible to Luis and gave him the same pep talk and direction. We prayed a bit more. We talked a lot more.

"How come you're not afraid of going back to El Salvador?" he asked. "After all these years, that has to be like going to a foreign country."

"I don't know, man. I'm leaving it in God's hands. I can tell you that I don't know what I'm going to do when I get down there. I'm going to have to trust in God, just like I'm telling you to place your trust in Him. It's the same thing."

Within moments of telling him this, Agent Turner approached the bars. "Diaz, you have anything in this holding cell?"

This was it. Time to gather up my belongings and go.

"No, I don't."

"Step forward. It looks like we made a mistake."

I looked at him, very puzzled.

"We can't let you go home from here, but we're going to take you back to New Folsom, and they'll parole you from there."

Miguel and Luis couldn't believe what they just heard. Neither could I.

"I thought you said you weren't born here," Miguel said.

"I wasn't. I don't know what to tell you except that God is not done with me here. That's all I can say."

Within minutes, the gate opened, and I was let out of the metal holding tank. I followed Agent Turner down a long corridor where the transportation vans were located, the same corridor I walked through when they brought me in there. As we were walking, he said, "Diaz, can I ask you a question?"

"Sure."

"What happened in that holding cell?"

"I led those two guys to Christ."

He stopped walking and looked at me. "I've been working here as a federal agent for more than twenty years. Every time I pick up guys that we're going to deport and see them carrying Bibles, I know they are going to be phonies. You know why I say that? Because every single time I put them in the holding tank, within seconds or minutes, I can hear their conversations on the phone. They're always talking to their buddies about what girl they are going to sleep with or who they're going to get high with when they get deported. It's like they played that religious game, and now they can put the Bible aside. But what you did is something I've never seen happen in the twenty years I've been doing this."

"Thanks, sir. That means a lot, coming from someone like you."

"Here's another thing," Agent Turner said. "I'm a Christian as well. I've never seen anyone lead someone to Christ like that in the tank, and especially not two prisoners. That was amazing what you did."

At the end of the corridor, I saw several black milk crates stacked on the linoleum floor. I was familiar with those crates. They held the chains for the hands and waist.

We stopped. I knew what had to happen next: I had to be chained up for the return trip to New Folsom.

When Agent Turner reached for the handcuffs and looked in my direction, I could see that his eyes were real watery. I was moved because this was a federal agent reacting emotionally—a hardened federal agent who had seen it all—to the situation we all found ourselves in.

"You don't deserve these chains," he said. "I don't know why I'm telling you this, but I feel guilty putting these chains on you." His voice cracked with emotion, and his eyes still watered.

I put my hands out so he could put the cuffs on me. "Don't worry about it," I said. "You're just doing your job."

After the cuffs came the restraints and chain around my waist. Then he loaded me into the same INS van. This time he was by himself. No partner. We both knew that I was going to be a free man within a matter of hours, so it would be stupid of me to try anything.

◆　　◆　　◆

During the long drive back to state prison, Agent Turner asked me to tell him my story. I shared my testimony—what God had done in the SHU and how I came to Christ. I described the green light on my life, the persecution I had to go through. I told him everything.

As I recounted the story I've shared in this book, Agent Turner started crying. I mean, he was weeping. There were tears running down his cheeks.

I tried to lighten the mood. "Hey, man, I need to stop telling you my story because you could get into an accident, and then I'll never get home."

We shared a chuckle. As he pulled off the main road and into the grounds of New Folsom, he had a question. "When you get out, would you be willing to share your story with some of the agents in my office?"

"Really?" I couldn't imagine a bunch of INS agents wanting to listen to an ex-con.

"Yeah, it would bring much hope. A lot of the agents here are born-again Christians. It wears us down when we see so much hypocrisy when inmates walk out holding Bibles and T-shirts with Bible verses, all for show. Hearing your story would bring a whole lot of faith and a whole lot of belief that people can change, and change in an authentic way. Would you be willing to do that?"

"Absolutely," I replied. "I don't have a car or anything, so I don't know how I would get to you, but if somehow I could, I absolutely would love to do that."

When he dropped me off at New Folsom, I really felt like a free man . . . although I still hadn't been officially released. It was nearing ten o'clock at night, so I had a feeling that it was too late to drive me to a train station or a bus depot.

I was taken to an office and told to wait. Then a correctional officer entered and confirmed my thoughts: I would have to spend one more night at New Folsom.

"We can't put you in mainline because we couldn't guarantee your safety," Agent Turner said. "If you were to die or something bad would happen to you, there would be big trouble, so we're going to put you in solitary. It's just one more night. First thing in the morning, we'll release you. Promise."

I couldn't carry my box of belongings because I was still in chains, so two guards escorted me through a series of corridors that became more and more familiar. And then I recognized where we were—the Security Housing Unit where I had been incarcerated upon my arrival at New Folsom nearly six years earlier.

I didn't say a word, however. I just followed the lead guard.

He opened a door and led me to the end of the SHU. This was exactly where I had been locked up in solitary. He reached for his keys and opened the door—to the *exact same cell*!

I had never felt happier. This was the same cell where I experienced freedom. This was the same cell where I went from being imprisoned by sin to being set free from all the junk in my life. It was like God telling me, *This is where you and Me first talked. This is where I delivered you.*

I stepped inside my cell, and the guards freed me from my chains. I felt a wonderful release in my heart and punched the air in victory. Then I lay down on my old bed to contemplate what had just happened. That's when I spotted the holes in the ceiling and started counting. Yup, the number was the same: 3,680.

I read my Bible. I stood up and did jumping jacks. I praised God for saving me from the fires of hell, and then I fell fitfully asleep.

When I woke up, I reminded myself that I would be leaving New Folsom as a free man—today.

chapter fifteen

A SURPRISE VISITOR

I didn't expect the California Department of Corrections and Rehabilitation to leave a mint on my pillow for my last night in prison, but I thought I'd at least get a ride to the Greyhound bus depot in downtown Sacramento.

Instead, six guys and I were dropped off in the middle of nowhere, out in the tulies, at a light rail stop.

"Good luck," one of the correctional officers said. "You want to go that way." He jerked his thumb to the left.

It was around eight o'clock in the morning. The date: July 3, 1995. I was twenty-three years old.

We eventually figured things out and hopped on the light rail car for a forty-five-minute ride to downtown Sacramento, California's capital city. Then it was a short walk to the Greyhound bus depot.

I can't remember exactly how long it took to ride a Greyhound to Los Angeles, but it was more than twelve hours. When I arrived in downtown LA, I caught a local bus to 3rd and New Hampshire in

Koreatown, where my parents lived in an apartment. Yes, they were still together after all those years. I should add that I had zero relationship with my father. He never wrote me, I never spoke to him on the phone, and as far as I was concerned, we were strangers.

One of the great joys in my life, though, is recalling how my mother squealed with delight when she answered my knock on the door. It was a special moment when she fell into my arms, a jumble of tears and cries of sheer happiness.

I'll admit that I took it easy during my first week of freedom. But there was something else I wanted to do, and that was to thank Frances Proctor in person for everything she had done for me.

That is, after I surprised her.

The following Sunday morning I got up early to take a series of bus rides to Triedstone Missionary Baptist Church on the border of Compton and South-Central LA. I arrived a bit early for the 9:30 service, so I killed time in a bakery by eating a chocolate glazed doughnut. Munching on sweet treats any time I wanted—day or night—had been a happy perk since my release a week earlier.

Triedstone Missionary Baptist, on West Adams, was located in a very old building. When I walked in the back door, my goal was to find Frances Proctor and sit next to her. I didn't see her initially. The church was full—practically every seat in the small church was taken. I'd say the church held 150 to 200 people.

I caught the eye of an usher lady who had to be at least one hundred years old. She beckoned me to follow her, but I didn't want to cause any commotion. I motioned that I would just stand in the back. But she waved her bony arm like a windmill and urged me to follow her. As she slowly worked her way up the center aisle, I saw a sea of black faces turning to look at me.

I'm sure the fact that I was the only non–African American in the building and was wearing typical Latino gang clothes—baggy Levi's jeans with baby cuffs, a wide black belt, a creased white T-shirt, and heavy boots—had something to do with it. The hair on my head was shaved short, which was another giveaway.

As we advanced farther into the church sanctuary, the congregants in each row turned to see what the commotion was all about, which prompted those in the next row up to turn in my direction. This continued until nearly everyone in the church was looking at me.

Then the youth director—a nice lady I recognized as being part of the prison outreach team to New Folsom—made eye contact with me. She was sitting in the front row on the right side of the church. She nudged the person next to her, who nudged the person next to her, and so forth, until she got the attention of Frances Proctor, who was seated in the front row on the *left* side of the church.

Frances looked back, and when she saw me, I thought she was going to faint. She caught herself, then waved an arm to come join her. Room was made for me to squeeze in and sit beside this living saint. We exchanged a warm hug.

By now we had totally disrupted the service, but the pastor and deacons on the stage rolled with things. One of the laypersons was Deacon Crockett, also part of the prison ministry team. He approached the pulpit and raised his arms.

"I see that we have Darwin Diaz in the house," he said, pointing toward me. "Come up here, young man. You, too, Frances."

As applause rained down, my eyes filled with tears as Deacon Crockett wrapped his beefy arm around my shoulder. He then proceeded to tell the congregation the story of how Frances walked into the SHU with the prison team to offer encouragement and hope to me and other prisoners in solitary confinement.

My cell, Deacon Crockett said, was blocked when the door leading into the SHU was opened. Consequently, no one knew there was a cell there until the time Frances spotted it. She asked a guard if there was a man in that cell.

"The guard said, 'Yeah, but that's Diaz. You don't want to know him,'" Deacon Crockett said. "But Frances told the guard, 'Oh, no. I *do* want to know him.' She told Darwin that she was going to pray for him and that God would do something powerful with his life. And now look at Brother Darwin. He gave his life to Christ three years ago and began leading *other* prisoners to Christ. Now our brother has been released, and we rejoice that he's in our midst today!"

I heard applause and shouts of "Hallelujah!" and "God be praised!" I'll admit that I got choked up. I couldn't raise my head and look at the congregation because I didn't want the tears welling in my eyes to stream down my face. I took a moment to wipe my damp eyes and then I looked up . . . and what I saw in those happy faces—faces full of joy for me—was an incredibly exciting moment for me.

And it all happened because an older black woman told me that she was praying for me and that Jesus was going to use me.

I knew that Jesus had used me inside New Folsom. Now that I was free—and had been paroled four years early—I wondered how He was going to use me on the outside.

✦　✦　✦

I didn't think it would be a good idea to show myself around my old neighborhood in Koreatown, so I exercised some wisdom: I decided to start rebuilding my life in San Pedro, a working-class port city next to the Los Angeles Harbor and twenty-five miles south of downtown LA. I needed a job, and I figured there was some type of dockworker or blue-collar job that I could pick up and build on.

I found a cheap apartment and moved in. I didn't have any money left over to buy a car, but I figured I was central enough that I could walk or take a bus to work or wherever I needed to go. While I pounded the pavement looking for a job, I kept a lookout for a church to join, which was an even bigger priority for me.

How would I find a good church in a small city of eighty-five thousand where I knew absolutely no one? In those days, the mid-1990s, I didn't have any clue about a recent invention called the internet, but it wouldn't have mattered since I didn't have a computer and churches didn't have websites back then. Smartphones weren't around yet either, which meant there was no Yelp or NextDoor app that I could tap into.

Instead, I looked for a church the old-school way: I found a phone booth—there were still plenty around back then—that had a Yellow Pages. I ripped out the "Church" section of the Yellow Pages—yes, I knew I wasn't supposed to do that, but I did it anyway—and took the sheaf of pages back to my apartment. With a city map on my lap, I looked up the locations of churches within walking distance.

Next, I wrote out a dozen and a half letters that said this:

To Whom It May Concern:
  I just got out of prison. I'm looking for a church. I'm living in an apartment in San Pedro, and I was wondering if I could sit down with someone who could tell me about your church so that maybe I can join it.

I included my address and the number of the phone in my apartment for the church to contact me. For the next week, as I walked around San Pedro looking for Help Wanted signs, I stopped at various churches and placed letters into at least fifteen mailboxes.

One midweek afternoon, I passed a church where I heard music playing. I decided to investigate. I approached the entrance and looked inside. In the front was a band practicing for the Sunday services. I looked to my right and left and saw only one person in the back—a middle-aged man.

I caught his eye and walked over to him. "Hi, my name is Casey. How's church here?"

He looked me up and down, then said, "I guess you're going to have to show up to find out." And then he turned on his heels and walked away from me.

In other words, he dissed me.

None of the churches I wrote tried to contact me, which hurt my spirit. This wasn't what church was like on the inside. We were a brotherhood behind prison walls. We broke bread together, and we risked our lives together. Church inside prison was almost like church from the book of Acts. We were that close and that involved with each other's lives. *If someone falls, you pick him up.* That was our mind-set.

Okay, maybe I didn't exercise much wisdom in starting my letter with the sentence, "I just got out of prison." Still, the lack of response was quite a blow. In fact, when the dude in the back of the church blew me off like that, I'll admit that some of the old me wanted to come out and give him some hard candy.

Instead, I swallowed the disappointment and returned to my threadbare apartment, where I read my Bible and prayed about what to do next. I decided that the first thing I needed to do was get a haircut.

There was a barbershop around the corner, manned by a single barber. Someone was getting his hair cut when I walked in, so I sat down and picked up the morning newspaper while I waited my turn. Then another guy a bit older than me entered the barbershop and took a seat two chairs from me.

As I scanned my newspaper, I had a feeling that I was being watched. When you've been in prison as long as I had, you develop a sixth sense about people, especially anyone checking you out. Every time I glanced up from my newspaper and looked over at him, he averted his eyes. I knew he was checking me out.

I didn't want to be confrontational. I just knew he was looking at me. I was about to say something when—

"When did you touch down?" he asked.

Touch down. Now there was prison slang if I ever heard it. *When did you touch down?* meant *When did you get out of prison?*

I looked at him. "How did you know I just got out?"

"You're still wearing your prison boots," he replied.

I glanced down. "You're right. Fair enough."

"It's all good," he said soothingly. "Where are you living?"

"Around the corner."

"What are you up to?"

"Finding a job. I have thirty days, according to the parole board."

"Any luck?"

"Not yet. I'm still looking for a job and for a church."

"You're looking for a church?"

"Yeah," I said, and then I told him about the letters that I had been dropping into the church mailboxes and what they said.

He laughed. "Maybe you shouldn't have put, 'I just got out of prison.'"

"Maybe you're right," I grinned.

"I'm a believer too. Why don't you come to our church? We're having a midweek service tonight at 7:30. It's only a few blocks from here."

We agreed to meet in front of the barbershop at seven o'clock, and sure enough, he was there on time and escorted me to Risen Son Ministries, a storefront church. Everything was great. I was used to God supernaturally putting things in front of me when I was inside, so I felt encouraged that He led me to this church following the disappointment of receiving no responses from the churches I had contacted. *Okay, God, we're back in tune here. All right, I see what You're doing.*

Risen Son, a multicultural church, was filled with friendly folks and a lot of young adults. After a few Sundays, though, my Uncle Rene called and offered me a job installing hardwood floors. He said he'd train me and that I could even live in a "granny flat" in the backyard of his Los Angeles home. He'd give me a good deal on rent, he said, since I was getting back on my feet.

✦   ✦   ✦

Uncle Rene Araujo was married to my mom's sister, Isabelle. A successful businessman, Uncle Rene had a nose for making money. Everything he touched seemed to turn to gold. He owned several properties and had a prosperous hardwood flooring business. He was living the American Dream—but he didn't believe in God. He didn't like God. He didn't want to have anything to do with God.

One time I accompanied Uncle Rene to the bank. He had several big checks to deposit. On the drive over, I shared my testimony and witnessed to him, but he waved me off. "I understand how you need God because of the stuff you did, but I don't believe in God. Everything that I own came from my own hands."

From the driver's seat of his late-model truck, he stretched out his right hand. "See, this is what made me. My hands. My hard work. That is why I own what I own and why I get to enjoy what I enjoy. It has nothing to do with God."

"Suit yourself, Uncle Rene." I wasn't about to press him since he made it clear that his heart wasn't open to the gospel. That said, I deeply appreciated him taking me in and teaching me a trade.

I got settled and found a nice but not-too-large evangelical church in Eagle Rock, a Los Angeles suburb located between Pasadena and Glendale and south of the 134 freeway. Almost immediately I met a young woman who was absolutely beautiful inside and out. Sana Halaby was her name.

She looked like an olive-skinned white woman from Kentucky, but she was the daughter of Lebanese immigrants. As we got to know each other, it turned out that we had a lot in common. Two months before my release, Sana walked out of a federal prison in Dublin, California, where she had served a twenty-seven-month prison term for being part of a major drug ring. She found Christ in prison as well.

We volunteered to be part of the youth ministry and became fast friends. I didn't have the courage to date her for two and a half years, but she also kept me at arm's length. I was okay with that because I saw her doing the same thing to a bunch of guys who wanted to take her out. Since I didn't really know much about the "rules of engagement" when it came to dating, I took the situation to the Lord in prayer. He told me to keep my distance and just get to know her while I helped her with the youth ministry.

As I got to know her and her heart better, I could see that she was someone special. I started fasting three, four days a week—water only—until I felt the Lord tell me that I could date her. I had fasted before and studied what fasting does. It seems like every time I fasted about certain things going on in my life, good things would happen.

After eight months of regular fasting, I felt like I got the green light from the Lord to call her. "I like you, but I don't want to get shot down like the rest of the guys, so let's clear the smoke right now," I said. "I don't want to date if this isn't going to head toward marriage."

Sana liked my boldness. "Okay, let's see what happens," she said.

Well, that's all both of us needed to spend time together and see if we were a match. As our love grew, I knew she was the special one for me. I proposed to her at church, and we were married on July 3, 1999, exactly four years to the day that I left New Folsom prison.

Our first daughter, Samantha, arrived thirteen months later on August 14, 2000. A second daughter, whom we named Miah, announced herself on October 24, 2001. Life was good and was full. During this time, I stopped working for my uncle and made a career change into the security industry.

I have no idea how I passed a background check, but a bank hired me to do security. Then I got a break when Dreamworks, an animation studio founded by film director and producer Steven Spielberg, former Disney executive Jeffrey Katzenberg, and music executive David Geffen, hired me to be part of their security team. I quickly rose to become head of security and was put in charge of a hundred guys.

Security—and fighting piracy—was a big deal at an animation studio that produced hits like *Antz, Shrek, Shark Tale,* and *Madagascar.*

✦ ✦ ✦

Sana and I volunteered to put on a music event for the youth at the church we were attending. The church was so small that there was no budget for a three-foot-by-ten-foot banner that would have cost four hundred dollars. We still needed a nice sign, so I got some white butcher paper, a set of Sharpies, and several markers and made our own banner.

The drummer of the band playing that night—a guy named Todd Moriarity—saw my handiwork. He owned a sign shop and knew a good banner when he saw one. He told me he thought I had some talent and took an interest in me and offered to teach me the sign business. I interned with him for two years while I held on to my security job at Dreamworks, which means I got very little sleep. Todd not only gave me hands-on training on how to produce banners and signage but also taught me the business side of running a sign shop.

After two years, a fellow named Vernon McKee—who mentored Todd in making signs—wanted to retire and sell his sign shop business. We worked out a deal for me to take over his business, which I named Samiah Signs—a mash-up of my daughters' first names. In the last few years, we have found a niche as a sign-maker for the TV and movie industry. Our signs can be seen in the background of TV shows like *Criminal Minds* and Netflix series like *Malibu Rescue* and *Glow.* We have dozens of great accounts, so God has blessed us mightily.

✦ ✦ ✦

There is one other major event I should mention. Around ten years ago, Sana and I learned we were having a "surprise baby." A son named

Jacob joined our family on September 16, 2008, and he shares the same birthday as Sana.

At the time of Jacob's birth, Sana and I had started a church known as Fresh Bread Christian Fellowship in Burbank. I was the pastor and loved preaching on Sundays, but our church needed a full-time pastor at the helm. In 2017, we merged with a multicultural church called Worshipwalk with Joe Hernandez as the senior pastor. I stepped into the role of community pastor, which means I was put in charge of overseeing the small-group Bible studies and discipleship training. These days, I pitch in wherever I'm needed, from preaching when Joe is on vacation to waxing the floors.

Don't forget: no one can make a floor shinier than I can.

♦   ♦   ♦

As I look back at what God's done in my life, I am absolutely amazed at the grace He's given me and the opportunities He's bestowed on me to share the gospel. My life is a miracle in many ways, and I give all glory and honor to Him.

The key message I want to end with is the importance of intercessory prayer. The only reason I'm able to share my story of redemption in *The Shot Caller* is because a little old black lady who didn't know me from Adam interceded on my behalf and prayed fervently that the Creator of the universe would touch my life. Without Frances Proctor lifting me up before the throne of God, I'd be dead or still in prison. I'm sure of that.

Think about what she did because I was *not looking* for God when I was in the SHU. I had only been in a church a handful of times in my life, so I barely knew who God was. I had never heard the message of John 3:16 that God so loved this world that He sent his only begotten Son and that whoever believes in Him shall not perish but have eternal life. I had never held a Bible in my hands, let alone seen one, so I didn't know who Jesus was or why He was the Messiah.

Consider the sacrifices that Frances made just to be able to get inside the solitary confinement wing of New Folsom State Prison. She and her team drove all day—more than eight hours—from Los Angeles to Folsom, and spent the night in a hotel. Then the Triedstone Baptist team did their prison ministry the next day and drove all the way back to Los Angeles, leaving in the late afternoon and arriving at midnight. Yet Frances willingly gave up two days every month to be the feet and hands of Jesus, reaching out to prisoners and sharing the good news.

And then in the SHU, my cell was the last one in the block and partially blocked by a door. Yet she was inquisitive enough to ask, "Is there a man in that cell?"

When told yes, she approached my gate and said, "I'm praying for you, and I believe God is going to use you."

My initial reaction was to laugh, but Frances wasn't fazed or discouraged by my scornful reply. In her prayer time, she lifted up my name and asked God to work a mighty miracle in my life.

And look what happened.

Frances Proctor and I remain in contact today. She resides in Austin, Texas, living out her golden years. Her six sons have become pastors in the Los Angeles area. Since I've become a pastor, we joke that she has seven sons in the pulpit.

◆ ◆ ◆

I want to finish with one more story. This concerns my Uncle Rene, the self-made millionaire who told me that he didn't believe in God or need God.

About six years ago, I received a phone call from Aunt Isabelle who relayed some sad news: Uncle Rene had an aggressive form of pancreatic cancer, stage IV. Doctors gave him only a few weeks to live.

I desperately wanted to share the gospel one more time with him. Uncle Rene was on the doorstep of eternity, and he wasn't saved.

I was praying about what to say to Uncle Rene, but I heard the Lord saying: *Don't go yet.* So I didn't visit him, even though all his family members were spending time with him, knowing that the time was short.

For two weeks, I was a no-show, which was a cause for distress in the family. *Where's Casey? How come he's not here to see his uncle before he dies?*

Finally, God released me to go there to see him. When I arrived at his house, his son, Alan, greeted me at the door. A dozen family members were milling about.

Inside the living room, my uncle was lying across a fluffy couch. He looked like a skeleton and weighed about eighty pounds. The bones on his face looked like they were going to protrude through his skin. His head lay in the lap of one of his sisters, and his other sister was at his feet, massaging them. Uncle Rene looked like he was near the end.

I pulled my cousin aside. "Hey, I need a few minutes by myself with your dad, and I think you know why."

Alan looked at me. "How am I going to do that?" he whispered, nodding toward his aunts on the couch and the relatives seated in chairs.

"Just find a way to do it. It's very important!"

I decided to step outside of the house to give the family some privacy. Ten minutes later, Alan came and got me. "You can speak to him now."

When I went back in their house, the aunts helped me walk Uncle Rene—by very carefully taking hold of his arms—to his bedroom. From the disapproving looks that I received from other family members, I could tell they didn't agree with what I had asked for, but I wasn't concerned about their feelings. Where Uncle Rene would spend eternity was at stake.

We slowly led my uncle to his bedroom and laid him down on his bed. I turned to my aunts and cousin and said, "Can I be alone with him for a few minutes?"

They quietly departed.

I sat down on Uncle Rene's bed.

"Uncle Rene, I know you've done a lot of good on this earth and in this life. I want to thank you for giving me a chance and for giving me a job when no one else would," I began. "I know it was kind of hard when my parole officer would show up at the job site at the most inopportune moments, but you were okay with that."

Uncle Rene looked at me and nodded for me to continue. He was listening.

"Here's the deal," I said. "According to Scripture, for all the good that you have done, the Bible says it's nothing but filthy rags. Our good deeds can't get us to heaven. That is the reality. In God's eyes, whatever you have done in your life is just as bad as what I have done in my life. You might not see it that way, society might not see it like that, but God sees it that way because sin is sin and that is just the bottom line."

I paused to let my words sink in.

"Look at how God has been merciful to you," I explained. "He loves you so much that He has allowed you to live long enough for me to get here and for us to sit down and have this moment. Don't let this last opportunity to repent and call out to God to forgive you pass by. This cancer is nothing. It's like a papercut compared to eternity in hell for rejecting the Son of God. Going to hell is forever! You will be in fire. You will be in complete punishment forever and ever and ever. But God loves you so much that He sent me here today—to talk to you."

I was on a roll, and I wasn't about to back down.

"Remember the time when we were going to the bank and you were telling me about all the properties you owned and the money you had and you said, 'My hands have done this'? Your hands have done nothing. God gave you the strength, the wisdom, and the ability to create business and make you wealthy. God put that inside of you, and you gave Him no credit. But here's the deal: Again, I am telling you, God loves you. He is giving you this last opportunity to repent and ask for forgiveness and to allow the Son of God to dwell in your heart."

I looked to see if anything I was saying was registering in his heart. I could tell from the look in his eyes that my words were finding their mark. My uncle was ready. "Would you like to come to Christ?" I asked.

"Yes, I would!" he replied.

I clasped my hands. "Great! Let's pray and ask God for forgiveness and give your life to Christ right now. We don't want to waste another moment."

We held hands, and I led Uncle Rene through the sinner's prayer. When we came to the "amen" at the end, he was in tears.

Uncle Rene looked at me. With his voice cracking, he said, "Darwin, I have never felt so much at peace. I missed it all this time. You were right, I missed it. But now I feel this tremendous peace."

I smiled. Uncle Rene had always called me Casey, but I wasn't going to ask him why he called me Darwin, not at this moment.

"Uncle Rene, you are born again. The Spirit of the living God has come into you. Remember: He shed His blood for you. All your sins have been forgiven, every last one. Now you know that the second you die, you are going to heaven. You are going to see Jesus. Scripture says to be absent from the body is to be present with the Lord. The second you die, you are going to see Jesus. You are going to be in paradise forever. I am actually kind of jealous because you are going to see Him before I do."

We chuckled about that, but what a great moment. We hugged and Uncle Rene wept some more. Then I looked at him and thought, *God, thank You for getting my uncle into heaven at the last moment.*

Two days later, Uncle Rene looked into the eyes of Jesus.

Once again, I was reminded of Psalm 103:15 (KJV): "As for man, his days are as grass: as a flower of the field, so he flourisheth."

No truer words were ever said.

chapter sixteen

KEEPING KIDS OUT OF GANGS

I understand that there will be many parents drawn to my story because they are worried that their teens—boys and girls—could be drawn to the gang life.

If you're feeling that way, I understand your concern. May I remind you that it's personal to me as well. I have two teenage girls and a boy who is ten years old—right about the time I first came into contact with the gang culture. I know firsthand how gangs destroy lives and ravage neighborhoods. I was caught up in that destructive lifestyle and was in about as deep as you can go. I most likely would not be alive today if I had not been arrested and sent to prison.

I'd say the biggest difference between the eighties—when I was a teenager—and today is that gangs are much more prevalent, much more widespread, and much more dangerous than they were in my day. Gang membership has increased by as much as 40 percent in the United States in recent years, and an estimated 1.4 million people are active in more than thirty-three thousand street, prison, and outlaw motorcycle gangs across the country, according to a "National Gang Threat Assessment" issued by the FBI.

Criminal street gangs have become one of the most serious crime problems in this country. Assaults, drive-by shootings, homicides, and brutal home-invasion robberies account for the single largest threat to personal safety in the United States. Gangs are responsible for nearly half of the nation's violent crimes.

Gang violence in El Salvador, the country of my birth, as well as Honduras and Guatemala has driven an uninterrupted exodus of desperate migrants, including entire families, through our porous southern border. Accompanying them are gang members who see an opportunity to bring their savagery to this country. The most notorious is MS-13, a gang that originated in El Salvador and that has established a heavy presence in Los Angeles, San Francisco, Houston, New York City, Washington DC, and urban areas of New Jersey.

What is new about gangs like MS-13, at least compared to my day, is how these gangs have gone heavily into human and child trafficking. It breaks my heart when I think of the young girls forced into sexual slavery to quench the thirst of perverted individuals.

I've met with and spoken to thousands of parents over the years about how to keep their children out of gangs. There is no easy answer or surefire panacea, but you can certainly take steps to greatly reduce the odds of one of your children being caught up in a gang. Here is a list of some ideas to keep in mind followed by explanations for each suggestion.

- Gangs recruit the very young, so be on the lookout.
- Pay attention to the clothes your children wear, what's in their pockets, and what they're saying on social media.
- Explain the consequences of being in a gang.

- Ask yourself what type of role model you are.
- Be thinking about your work-life balance.
- If you're a single-parent mom, realize that you have the toughest assignment possible.
- Paint over any graffiti in the neighborhood.
- Take an interest in your children's sports or hobbies.
- Encourage academic success.
- Be approachable as a parent.
- If your child is already in a gang, there's still hope.

GANGS RECRUIT THE VERY YOUNG, SO BE ON THE LOOKOUT

I was ten years old when I started hanging out with the wrong crowd. When I was an elementary school kid, fifteen-year-old Pedro Arroyo introduced me to gang life and jumped me into Rockwood when I was eleven.

Now, the fact that a fifteen-year-old boy was taking an interest in an eleven-year old kid should tell you something right away. If my young son, Jacob, started hanging out with someone five or six years older than him, that would be a major cause for concern because fifteen- and sixteen-year-olds don't normally want to hang around school kids—unless there's something in it for them.

For Pedro Arroyo, bringing me into the gang was a way to bolster his numbers and have another kid at his disposal to steal, rob, and maim other gang members. If one of your children is tagging along with someone a half dozen years older—which is quite a physical difference and a big maturity gap—then that's a big sign that your child is being influenced by a gang member. You must do everything you can to prevent your child from joining a gang because that's *their* goal—to take your child away from you.

PAY ATTENTION TO THE CLOTHES YOUR CHILDREN WEAR, WHAT'S IN THEIR POCKETS, AND WHAT THEY'RE SAYING ON SOCIAL MEDIA

Gangs distinguish themselves by their "colors," which represent their neighborhoods. The Crips, a black gang in LA, wear blue or black or a combination of the two. Their archrivals, the Bloods, wear red. The Latin Kings wear black and gold. Ball caps and bandanas are also used to identify gang members.

"Wearing the colors" isn't as prevalent today because gang members want to avoid being easily identified by police and witnesses. But if your kid is wearing a handkerchief out of a back pocket or a generic ball cap that's not representing a team from a major sport or a college football or basketball team, that could be a sign that he's flashing his colors or at least sympathetic to a local gang.

Young kids can't get tattoos, but if you have a sixteen- or seventeen-year-old who can pass for eighteen and is suddenly sporting a gang-identifying tattoo, then alarm bells should go off. You have a major problem and need help from counselors and youth pastors.

Finally, be aware of what your teens are saying on their Facebook pages and Instagram and Twitter accounts. Social media is what many today use to declare themselves gang members or sympathetic loyalties to a certain gang.

EXPLAIN THE CONSEQUENCES OF BEING IN A GANG

I understand that very few parents will be able to share with their children just how dangerous it is to be involved in a gang the same way I can. But go ahead and "scare them straight." Share this book with them if it's age appropriate. Let them see that becoming involved in a gang almost always results in one of two things: death or incarceration.

Even if you don't get killed, being locked up with other gang members is far from a Sunday picnic. I came very close to being killed in prison. Living in fear for my life was a horrible existence. Show them how being involved with a gang will ruin their future and likely result in their destruction.

Gangs demand loyalty, but it's not a two-way street. I saw gang members turn their backs on their homies and kill them for the flimsiest of reasons. And the glamorous side of gang life—the easy money, the low-riding cars, and the girls—is all a mirage. If truth be known, the shot callers take the largest cut from the stolen goods, so the "spoils" are often not that much.

ASK YOURSELF WHAT TYPE OF ROLE MODEL YOU ARE

Your children need you to be a role model—a *good* role model. It's unbelievable how easily they are influenced. Kids are going to look to someone for guidance and advice and will make decisions based on what they think their role models would do.

You must be that role model. You must be that parent they can look up to. Model the kind of behavior that you want your kids to adopt because your children are paying attention to everything you say and do and will even imitate your words and actions. It's called "walking the talk."

If you talk about the importance of God in your life but rarely take the family to church, then your kids aren't going to believe you when you say you're a Christian. If you warn them about the dangers of drinking but are knocking down the beers during the football game and hollering at the TV over blown calls, then they're going to be naturally skeptical that you really mean what you say.

They say that values are "caught" rather than "taught." Let your kids catch you reading your Bible when they come out of their bedrooms in the morning. Let them catch you leaving the house to attend an early-morning Bible study. If your faith journey is still a work in progress, let your kids know that you have questions and are still figuring things out. That's okay as well. They will see you're being transparent and don't have all the answers.

Wherever you are, you need to be dependable. If you say that you're going to show up at their soccer games, be sure you arrive on time. If you promise to give them a treat for helping you rake up the fall leaves, be sure to take them out for a frozen yogurt sundae when the work is done. When you say you'll help them with their homework, turn off the TV and give them your undivided attention.

BE THINKING ABOUT YOUR WORK-LIFE BALANCE

If you're not around your kids, you can't be much of a role model. If you're not getting home until seven thirty or eight o'clock, their day is almost over. About all you can do is tuck them into bed.

I understand how companies are demanding more of their employees, including the hours they put into their jobs. But the best hours of the day for you—the parent—is from five o'clock in the afternoon until they go to bed. That's the sweet spot.

Anything you can do to be involved with your kids during their after-school hours is key. Maybe it means moving closer to work so as to cut down on your commute. Maybe it's seeing if you can work from home one or two days a week. Maybe it means taking a half-hour lunch instead of ninety minutes so that you can get more done during the day and leave work an hour earlier.

My mother had to work two jobs to keep our family afloat. Consequently, she was never around because she *couldn't* be around. Those were the cards she was given to play since my father's income was so sporadic. She did the best she could with the resources she had available at the time. I've had conversations with her in which she's been in tears, asking for forgiveness, and I've repeatedly assured her that what happened to me wasn't her fault. I don't blame her for anything or for the poor choices I made as a young man. We both know that if she had been able to be at home more while I was growing up, I wouldn't have caused her as much heartache as I did.

IF YOU'RE A SINGLE-PARENT MOM, REALIZE THAT YOU HAVE THE TOUGHEST ASSIGNMENT POSSIBLE

I understand how fractured the family is today. Single-parent moms not only have to earn enough money to pay for the basics (food, shelter, and transportation), but they have to be there for their kids as much as possible.

It's hard for a young mother to raise a man. Having a male presence in the home is not always possible due to divorce, disengagement, or disappearance, but this is where grandfathers and uncles can play a role, as well as male teachers and youth pastors.

Single-parent moms need to call in the reserves because of how difficult they have it when it comes to raising children. After-school programs, church youth groups, and sports leagues are great places to start.

PAINT OVER ANY GRAFFITI IN THE NEIGHBORHOOD

If you live in an area where buildings and fences are "tagged"—or if your home is hit—then doing the graffiti cleanup yourself will be an object lesson of how gang-related graffiti and claiming a neighborhood isn't cool. Perhaps if your teens participate in a neighborhood clean-up campaign with you, they will see how important it is to fight graffiti, which is used by gangs to mark their turf, advertise themselves, or claim credit for a crime.

TAKE AN INTEREST IN YOUR CHILDREN'S SPORTS OR HOBBIES

One of the best ways to stay in touch with your teen is to cheer them on if they are playing a sport or participate with them in one of their hobbies. Kids have a way of acting nonchalantly whenever a parent approaches them after a baseball game or volleyball match, as if your attendance in the grandstands didn't mean that much to them, but it does. They know when you are there and when you're not. When you offer praise for their play—or what I call appropriate admiration and not overly lavish compliments—they will sense how important they are to you. If your teens sense that you, as the parent, are the source of love, guidance, and protection in their lives, they won't go looking for these basic needs to be met by a gang.

ENCOURAGE ACADEMIC SUCCESS

It's amazing in how many precincts, especially in the inner city, it's not cool to study, not cool to get good grades, and not cool to buy into education. Yet everyone knows that strong study habits and a good education will take your kids places and are directly related to a young person's development.

Reward success in the classroom. Give them their favorite gift cards for bringing home a report card filled with good grades. Hand out compliments for completing their schoolwork and homework.

BE APPROACHABLE AS A PARENT

I'm taking this advice to heart. I have three kids, and one of the things I made sure early on was that my children knew I wasn't just there to put food on the table and a roof over their heads. I wasn't going to be the dad who was solely there to discipline. Sure, there were times when I had to assume that role, but I also wanted them to know that I'm always approachable. They can have my attention any time.

Here's an example: If I'm in the middle of a meeting and one of them calls me, then the meeting is going to stop. My children mean more to me than my business —more than anything in life. Outside of my relationship with Sana, I can't think of anything more important.

Kids love to do fun things, but they also like to be praised. I didn't have a parent patting me on the back and saying, "Good job, Casey." I didn't have someone assuring me that I could make it through this life, that they had my back.

That's why I'm focused on being approachable to my children. I want them to feel comfortable to come talk to me about anything—from sex to drugs to peer pressure to dealing with bullies.

Recently, a wonderful moment happened between me and my oldest daughter, Samantha. We were sitting in church together as a family when my seventeen-year-old leaned toward me and rested her head on my shoulder. I melted inside. Sam felt I was so approachable that she was comfortable enough to lay her head on my shoulder in a public setting.

Wow, God. You are so cool. Here is this teenager, and she still loves her dad.

I hope you get to enjoy wonderful parenting moments like that. You can by investing early and often in your children and making yourself available.

IF YOUR CHILD IS ALREADY IN A GANG, THERE'S STILL HOPE

All I have to do is look at myself and understand that anybody can be saved from the gang life. It starts with prayer—prayer that he or she will find Jesus (or come back to Him), make a U-turn, repent of his or her sins, leave the gang, and rebuild his or her life.

Teens generally won't leave a gang for their parents or because society tells them it's the right thing to do. Leaving a gang starts with a change of heart.

God is the one who can start all that. He's the Alpha and the Omega, the beginning and the end.

So while you still have breath, seek Him and ask Him to protect your children and give them no desire to get within hailing distance of a gang member.

You don't want them aspiring to be part of a gang. You want them aspiring to be like Jesus Christ, our Lord and Savior.

He is the real shot caller.

BIBLE VERSES THAT
SPOKE TO CASEY

The stranger who dwells among you shall be to you as one born among you, and you shall love him as yourself; for you were strangers in the land of Egypt: I am the LORD your God. (Leviticus 19:34)

My son, if sinners entice you, do not consent. (Proverbs 1:10)

If they say, "Come with us,
Let us lie in wait to shed blood;
Let us lurk secretly for the innocent without cause. . . ."
(PROVERBS 1:11)

My son, do not walk in the way with them,
Keep your foot from their path;
For their feet run to evil,
And they make haste to shed blood.
(PROVERBS 1:15–16)

But they lie in wait for their own blood,
They lurk secretly for their own lives.
(PROVERBS 1:18)

Therefore they shall eat the fruit of their own way,
And be filled to the full with their own fancies.
(PROVERBS 1:31)

"Agree with your adversary quickly, while you are on the way with him, lest your adversary deliver you to the judge, the judge hand you over to the officer, and you be thrown into prison." (Matthew 5:25)

But the wicked will be cut off from the earth,
And the unfaithful will be uprooted from it.
(PROVERBS 2:22)

"I was sought by those who did not ask for Me;
I was found by those who did not seek Me.
I said, 'Here I am, here I am,'
To a nation that was not called by My name."
(ISAIAH 65:1)

But the Lord said to him, "Go, for he is a chosen vessel of Mine to bear My name before Gentiles, kings, and the children of Israel. For I will show him how many things he must suffer for My name's sake." (Acts 9:15–16)

And the Lord added to the church daily those who were being saved. (Acts 2:47)

Remember the prisoners as if chained with them—those who are mistreated—since you yourselves are in the body also. (Hebrews 13:3)

He came to Nazareth where he had been reared. As he always did on the Sabbath, he went to the meeting place. When he stood up to read, he was handed the scroll of the prophet Isaiah. Unrolling the scroll, he found the place where it was written,

God's Spirit is on me;
he's chosen me to preach the Message of good news to
the poor,
Sent me to announce pardon to prisoners and
recovery of sight to the blind,
To set the burdened and battered free,
to announce, "This is God's year to act!"

(Luke 4:16-21 The Message)

However, Jesus did not permit him, but said to him, "Go home to your friends, and tell them what great things the Lord has done for you, and how He has had compassion on you." (Mark 5:19)

ACKNOWLEDGMENTS

In the summer of 2012, a friend of mine named Mical Pyeatt asked me to share my story—the one you've just read—to the managers at his successful financial services company.

At the time, I'd shared my "shot caller" story a number of times in public settings, but not a whole lot. The people who heard my testimony said they were moved by my story and that I should write a book, but I didn't know what to do with that.

Sitting around the table in a conference room that day, listening to my talk, Mical Pyeatt suddenly heard a Voice speak to him, saying, *I want you to help Casey get his story out.*

Mical—pronounced *Michael*—dismissed the thought out of hand.

Me, Lord? No way.

As I continued with my presentation, Mical heard God's voice again, but this time a bit firmer: *I want you to help Casey get his story out.*

Lord, I'm too busy. I have a wife and kids, a business, and no time.

Mical shrugged off the thought. A few minutes later, the Lord spoke to him again about helping me out.

Lord, I don't have any experience doing this.

But when he heard His voice a fourth time, Mical looked across the conference table at his wife, Sandra. He could tell that she was intently listening to me, totally engrossed in my story with tears rolling down both sides of her face.

And then Mical heard the Lord say a fourth time: *I want you to help this man get his story out.*

By now, what was he going to say? My friend submitted his will to God's, saying in his heart, *Okay, I will.*

Within forty-eight hours of saying yes to helping me—meaning, coming alongside to mentor and coach me as well as pick up some bills—spiritual attacks started. His personal life began to disintegrate, and there were challenges at work. Everything started coming apart at the seams. In a short time, his marriage of seventeen years blew up and the family broke apart. Mical went through an ugly divorce, and for a season he lost family, friends, health, home, belief, and all his personal confidence.

Throughout it all, Mical stuck by my side and has been the impetus behind this book and what I hope will be a full-length motion picture about my life someday. I am deeply grateful for what he's done for me.

There have been many people along the way who have been my bedrock and a huge source of encouragement. I start with my wife, Sana. With the greatest thankfulness to God, I acknowledge her indispensable contribution to my life. Sana has been a driving force in my life, from staying late at church while I help a family get back on their feet to starting a sign business with me and dealing with the struggles of owning a small business. She has done so willingly and without complaint, and I know she loves me just as I love her. I really mean it when I tell others that Sana fills my sails.

Not only has Sana given sacrificially of herself to me, but our children, Samantha, Miah, and Jacob, have endured long nights at church with never a peep of protest. It's not easy being pastors' kids—or being raised by two ex-convicts—but Samantha, Miah, and

Jacob have never acted embarrassed around us, which can happen with teenagers. I admire how they've stayed strong in the Lord, and their love and support have been evident to Sana and me and everyone around us.

Turning toward the writing of *The Shot Caller*, I must acknowledge and thank my collaborator Mike Yorkey, who took on this project without us ever knowing that it would see the light of publishing day. I had no money to get him started, but for two years, he worked on this book when he had some extra time or was between projects until *The Shot Caller* was completed. I'm amazed how Mike was able to take our numerous interviews and weave a compelling, captivating story, for which I'm deeply grateful. Early readers such as Heidi Moss, Ross Mitchell, and Nicole Yorkey provided important feedback.

I also want to thank Joel Kneedler, the publisher of Emanate Books, who saw the potential in *The Shot Caller* when no one else would in the Christian publishing industry. Joel is to be commended for taking a chance on me, but more than that, he's become a great friend in a short time. I also want to thank Forrest Smith, Joey Paul, and Janene MacIvor, who were early champions of *The Shot Caller* to become an Emanate Books title.

ABOUT THE AUTHORS

Darwin "Casey" Diaz is a native of El Salvador and a former gang leader. Growing up on the mean streets of Los Angeles, he was forced to fight for his life. He was eventually incarcerated as one of the most violent criminals in California and placed in solitary confinement. His life was forever changed in that cell when one day God approached Casey in a miraculous way. Upon his release from prison, Casey landed a job making signs and today runs his own company, Samiah Signs. Casey enjoys teaching at church and sharing his story with audiences around the country. Grateful for a second chance at life, Casey is now married to Sana and is the father of three children.

www.caseydiaz.net

Mike Yorkey is the author, coauthor, editor, or collaborator of one hundred books. He has written for the *Los Angeles Times* travel section, *Skiing*, *Tennis Week*, *World Tennis*, *City Sports*, and *Racquet*. He and his wife, Nicole, are the parents of two adult children and make their home in Encinitas, California.

www.mikeyorkey.com

INVITE CASEY TO SPEAK TODAY

Casey Diaz is a humble, thoughtful speaker with a passion to share how God can save anyone—including someone like himself after he was convicted of committing gang-related crimes and killing another gang member.

Casey is available to speak in church pulpits, men's and women's weekend conferences, and vacation retreats. If you, your church, or your community organization would like Casey to come speak at your event, contact him through his website at www.caseydiaz.com.

You can also follow him on social media:
website: caseydiaz.net
Facebook: Casey Diaz-Author
Instagram: caseydiaz#theshotcallerbook
Twitter: caseydiaz#theshotcallerBK